HOW TO WRITE A BOOK

How to get it published and how to get paid

by Calvin G. Sims, Sr.

"As a boy I loved to read. I read everything I could get my hands on. My favorite subject was history, especially the history of the "Old West." My problem was that neighborhood bullies, including my foster siblings would harass me unmercifully. They would hit me and take my books away and often destroy them. My solution was to climb into the large China Berry Tree that grew in my front yard. No one could see me there and I could read in peace."
...Calvin Sims

Calvin Sims is the Founder and Executive Director of CHINA BERRY TREE BOOKS. A division of StoryTellers of the American Frontier

DEDICATION

For My Dear Friend and Business Partner
My Mentor

Rachelle Riley

The world is waiting for your book

"It's none of their business that you had to learn to write. Let them think you were born that   way."
– *Ernest Hemingway*

CONTENTS

FOREWORD

I remember the first time I met a published author. It was at a Fall Festival in a park in Stone Mountain, Georgia.

The young black woman was standing behind a table with a stack of her books and other promotional materials. I was star struck.

I was 45 years old and she could not have been yet 30, but she was a published author. I had accomplished many things by that time in my life, but as long as I could remember I was most impressed and most wanted to join the ranks of writers.

Actually meeting her and observing the fact that she did not have wings nor a third eye in the middle of her head was encouraging. In other words, there was nothing, other than a difference in gender and age, about this woman that said that she had anything that I did not have.

If she can do it, I can too.

And though it took me almost 9 years after that to complete and publish my first book

("When the Student is Ready, the Teacher Will Appear; Trafford 2006), I look back on that moment as a watershed event in my writing career.

That is especially true because since my first book (I have published 12 as of this writing), I have had that same experience that she must have had upon encountering me.

I can feel it coming as I pause before responding to the question, "What do you do for a living?"

"I am a writer," I say.

The outward response from the inquirer will vary within a narrow range of from head to toe reassessment glances, to skeptical disbelief, to wide eyed amazement. What is likely to occur about 75% of the time is a variation of, "I want to write a book!"

Nine years after my encoder with the young female writer, things changed.

It was 2004 that I got serious.

Wallace "Wally" Amos was being interviewed on some TV show. He was talking about how he borrowed $25,000 from Marvin Gaye and Helen Reddy in 1975 and opened a cookie store to sell his "Famous Amos" brand of cookies. The story goes on to reveal that within a matter of 7 years, his revenue exceeded 12 million dollars.

Most significantly, Wally Amos was asked what advice he had for aspiring entrepreneurs. His advice changed my life. What is more, his advice became one of many mantras that would stay with me for the rest of my life.

He recounted how his cookie idea was nothing new to him in 1975 when he opened that first store, but something that he had wanted to do for over 10 years. He said that procrastination was the only reason that he had not done it sooner. His advice was simple.

"Do something, do it right now and do it every day."

He said that if it was nothing more than to design your logo, do something. "As soon as this program concludes, no matter where you are, do something. Grab a pencil and paper or even a napkin and make a list of what you need. Write down your goals. Just do it and do it now and do it every day!"

I started writing as soon as the program ended. I grabbed a noteBook and turned to a blank page where I wrote:

"When the Student is Ready, the Teacher Will Appear" by Calvin G. Sims

Two years later, I had a few pages and a title. I had the makings of a book; I just didn't know how to close the deal. A jumble of disjointed pages may well represent the ruminations of a talented mind, but who would want to read that? Furthermore, who would pay for the experience?

After two frustrating years of hitting and mostly missing at writing a book, I signed up for a "How to Write a Book" workshop.

As is the case with most workshops, the hardest thing was to stay awake as the presenters did their best to stretch the class out over the 3 days (24 hours) and thus justify the $1,500 that each student had to cough up in order to attend.

Don't get me wrong, the information that I came away with was well worth the price, it's just that it could have been disseminated in one session and not three.

Now that I knew how to write a book, I went home and quickly placed my manuscript into the trash (deleted it from my computer hard drive). The only thing I kept was the title; "When the Student is Ready, the Teacher Will Appear."

I started all over again using the techniques that I had just learned.

The book that I had been working on for two years was complete and ready to be submitted for publication in about 60 days.

I will never forget that blissful day when a box of books, written by me, arrived. In a scene that has been repeated a dozen times; I called for other family members to join me. We encircled the box as if we were about to open a magic oracle or something.

But instead of a magic oracle, the box contained several copies of a book that was written by me. From that moment forth I would be able to say with truth and pride that:

"I am a writer!"

The purpose of this, my 13th book, is to enable you to start that ritual of calling your family to gather around a box that was delivered.

A box that contains several copies of the book that was written by you.

GETTING STARTED

Defining the Physical Book

On TV, we often see a writer sit down at a typewriter and start to write something such as; "It was a cold, dark night in December...", and thus that is how he or she takes that first step toward writing a book. That is not the way a realistic presentation of the first steps towards writing a book.

The objective of your writing a book is its publication. It is for that reason that certain considerations must be taken at the onset of that creative process.

Since that book that is forming between your ears is eventually going to morph into something that you can hold in your hands and hopefully autograph for eager readers, there are certain decisions that have to be made. Decisions that will serve you best if they are made prior to the actual *writing.*

What Will Your Book Look Like?

Here is a technique for designing your book before you write it. You may or may not find this technique useful. Some writers do and some don't. The choice, as is the case with all of the suggestions herein, is all yours.

Here goes:

Decide what you want your book to look like. Purchase, borrow or check out from the library a book (or books) that is laid out like you want your book to look.

You are looking at the size (dimensions), the way each chapter starts, what is written at the top of the left side pages and the right side pages, the page numbers, the chapter headings. In other words, you want your book to look just like this book or books, in case you want some features from more than one book.

Determine what font (style and size) you will use and how many words will fit on a page.

HINT: Find a book that has a font that appeals to you, then count the number of words on several random pages in that book, then average that number to come up with the number of words per page.

<u>What Kind of Book Will It Be?</u>
Of course, there is the overarching choice between *fiction* and *nonfiction*.

<u>Fiction</u>
This category of literature refers to stories created from the imagination. The plot, settings and characters are all, generally created from the author's imagination.

The plot, settings and characters of a fictional story may also be based on actual events and/or persons. Still, the story is considered fiction if any elements of the story are created from imagination.

Several genres of fiction exist, such as:

- mysteries
- science fiction
- romance
- fantasy
- crime thrillers
- action and adventure

An example of classic fiction is my favorite book; *"To Kill a Mockingbird,"* by Harper Lee.

Other examples include:

- *"The Color Purple,"* by Alice Walker
- *"1984,"* by George Orwell
- *"Native Son,"* by Richard Wright
- *"Huckleberry Finn,"* by Mark Twain (the pen name of Samuel Langhorne Clemens)

<u>Nonfiction</u>
The nonfiction category of literature refers to stories based in fact.

Nonfiction is the broadest category of literature and may address such topics as, but not limited to:

biography
business
cooking
health and fitness
pets
crafts
home decorating
languages
travel
home improvement
religion

art
music
history
self-help
true crime
science
humor
even how to write a book

Nonfiction reports on true events. Histories, biographies, journalism, and essays are all considered nonfiction.

As a rule, nonfiction has a higher standard to uphold than fiction. A few instances of fact in a work of fiction does not make the entire work the truth, conversely, a few fabrications in a nonfiction work can force that story to lose all credibility.

Credibility is the foundation of nonfiction writing.

Some examples of classic nonfiction work are:

- *"The Autobiography of Malcolm X,"* by Alex Haley
- *"Think and Grow Rich,"* by Napoleon Hill or as adapted by Dennis Kimbro
- *"The 7 habits of Highly Effective People,"* by Stephen R. Covey
- *"I Know Why the Caged Bird Sings,"* by Maya Angelou
- *"Steve Jobs,"* by Walter Isaacson
- *"The Diary of a Young Girl,"* by Anne Frank
- *"Dreams From My Father,"* by Barack Obama
- *"Churchill,"* by Martin Gilbert
- *"The Taste of Country Cooking,"* by Edna Lewis
- *"Getting Things Done,"* by David Allen
- *"Windows 10,"* by Joe Goddard
- *"Dating for Dummies,"* by Joy Browne
- *"When the Student is Ready, the Teacher Will Appear,"* by Calvin G. Sims, Sr.

As you can see, nonfiction can span a virtually unlimited range of topics..

<u>What Would You Write a Fiction Book About?</u>

The sky is *not* the limit. In fact, there is *no* limit. As a fiction writer, you can let your imagination run wild.

You also have the option of taking some actual person place or event and using that person place or event as a springboard for your imagination.

An example may be a story of the secret romance between Cleopatra who really existed and a slave whose entire existence is the product of your imagination.

If you create a work of science fiction, you may want to pull out you physics text book and describe with accuracy how your nuclear powered space ship travels through space so quickly that it is able to traverse and explore previously unknown dimensions. The nuclear power source is based on reality, however, the amount of thrust that it is capable of is a product of your imagination applied to real science.

As a writer of fiction, you have the power to make flowers talk or create purple raindrops or an alien life form that has come to Earth to either cure all know disease or to eat us all. You have the power.

The power of imagination.

What Would You Write a Nonfiction Book About?

Should you decide to write a nonfiction book, you will need to identify sources of credible information on your subject.

If your book is a biography, you will need to list research material such as books written by or about your subject. Perhaps there are living family members or colleagues with whom you may conduct an interview.

If you choose to write about a famous person place or event, chances are that you will not be the first person to write about that topic. In fact, unless you are writing about a person place or event whose relevance is very recent, you can count on there being literary work created prior to your decision to explore the particular subject.

This is a good thing. Any work done prior to your work is a resource. There is absolutely nothing wrong with you rephrasing, interpreting or adding your point of view to work that has already been done.

To do so is *not* plagiarism.

I caution you here that it might be tempting to cut and paste work that has been done by others into your manuscript – DON'T DO IT!

That *is* plagiarism !

Plagiarism is against the law and can get you into serious trouble.

To avoid plagiarism when you gather information from published and or copyrighted material, simply state what you take away from what you've read in your own words. It is also a good idea to give credit to a publication that you may have found helpful.

There is also the option of seeking permission to reuse material in your book by contacting the publisher and following their procedure for including an excerpt from their owned intellectual property.

That collection of recipes that were handed down to you on 5 by 7 inch cards might make a wonderful cookbook. In which case you will probably not be required to get written permission from anyone and if so, the permission you seek will likely come from your mom, or hers.

Consider the book of photographs, all taken by you, or the collection of your own watercolors. Perhaps you have developed a special knitting stitch that combined with instructions can result in some amazing hand knit garments and accessories, as well as a very interesting 'How To' book.

Nonfiction writing can stretch from the serious to the whimsical. It can be used to solve all of the world's problems. It can launch a successful career by suggesting the development of a positive mental attitude. It can launch a political career that can lead all the way to the White House.

A book that instructs hobbyist to build a model airplane that can actually fly or a rocket that can climb several thousand feet before it deploys a parachute and slowly drifts back to Earth so that it can be refueled and launched again, and again, would be a work of nonfiction.

The following is a short list of a few of the many types of nonfiction books:

biography
history
handbooks and manuals
business
self-improvement
overcoming tragedy
first aid
LGBTQIA concerns
cooking
politics
marriage
dating
sex
electronics
gardening
pets
aquariums
moonshine
farming
herbal cures
text books
mining

selling
consumer protection
fishing
hunting
firearms
archery
sewing
journalism
philosophy
studying
walking
styling hair
make-up artistry
investment

While this list could have gone on and on, I hope you get the idea that a nonfiction book can be about just about anything so long as it is factual.

If the book is about growing roses, the reader must be able to follow the instructions in the book and grow roses for him or herself.

So choose your nonfiction topic, gather your facts together and you are well on your way to becoming a nonfiction author.

Size *Does* Matter

In the publishing or book printing industry, book sizes are known as trim sizes. The word 'Trim' refers to where the book is trimmed, usually during the final stage of production.

The options for book size vary greatly and with very few rules and limitations. There are, however, a number of conventions that are good to know about. (All sizes listed below are width by height.)

Trade paperbacks, a very popular category of books, are often in the 5-1/2" x 8-1/2" to 6" x 9" range. The 6" x 9" size has long been considered ideal for a book page.

You can create good looking books at different sizes but the majority of self-published books are trade paperbacks.

Manuals and workbooks are usually larger and, are in the 8" x 10" to 8-1/2" x 11" range. This size is also good for directories and instructional books with lots of graphics or detailed drawings.

This larger page size also lends itself to a 2-column text layout which is an efficient use of space.

Novels appear in lots of different sizes but smaller sizes seem to provide a more intimate reading experience. A smaller book in the range of 5-1/2″ x 8-1/2″ is probably the most popular size, but 5-1/4″ x 8″ is also a charming size for smaller novels. Longer novels move to 6″ x 9″ to avoid becoming overly bulky at smaller sizes.

The above rule for novels can be applied to:

- memoirs
- short story collections
- collections of essays

All depending on the size of the book.

General nonfiction titles seem to come out in 6″ x 9″ making this size arguably the most popular of all. It's also the most widely used size for hardcover books.

When more room is needed on the page, for instance for sidebars or pull quotes, 7″ x 10″ is a frequent solution.

Photography or art books don't conform to any particular size. They can be very small, or big and heavy 'coffee-table' books. Many artists and photographers prefer books that are square or nearly square. This allows both horizontal and vertical pictures to have about the same amount of white space on the page.

Here is the entire list of trim sizes offered by Lightning Source, the largest supplier of print on demand books:

4.37 x 7 inches (178 x 111mm)
4.72 x 7.48 inches (190 x 120mm)
5×7 inches (178 x 127mm)
5 x 8 inches (203 x 127mm)
5.06 x 7.81 inches (198 x 129mm)
5.25 x 8 inches (203 x 133mm)
5.5 x 8.5 inches (216 x 140mm)
5.83 x 8.27 inches (210 x 148mm)
6 x 9 inches (229 x 152mm)
6.14 x 9.21 inches (234 x 156mm)
6.625 x 10.25 inches (260 x 168mm)
6.69 x 9.61 inches (244 x 170mm)
7.44 x 9.69 inches (246 x 189mm)
7.50 x 9.25 inches (235 x 191mm)
7 x 10 inches (254 x 178mm)
8 x 8 inches (203 x 203mm)

8 x 10 inches (254 x 203mm)
8 x 10.88 inches (276 x 203mm)
8.25 x 11 inches (280 x 210mm)
8.268 x 11.693 inches (A4) (297 x 210mm)
8.5 x 8.5 inches (216 x 216mm)
8.5 x 9 inches (229 x 216mm)
8.5 x 11 inches (280 x 216mm)

Note that the **6 x 9 inches (229 x 152mm)** size is bold because, in addition to being the most popular trim size, it is the trim size most highly recommended for the majority of books.

Choosing a Size For Your Book

The vast majority of books that adorn the shelves of book stores are either 5-1/2″ x 8-1/2″ or 6″ x 9.″ These are good, readable sizes that work well for many types of books.

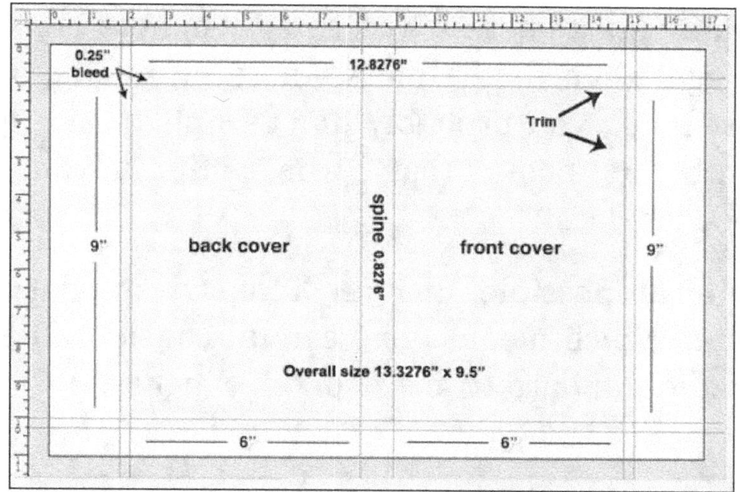

figure 1. 6 x 9 inch book cover layout

If this is your first book there is a good chance one of these two sizes will work for you.

Choose a different size if:

- your book is in a special category, such as a workbook
- there is a functional reason that you need a larger or smaller book, such as for a gift book or an atlas
- You want to stand out in your niche by having a different size than everyone else within that same niche.

Still, it is worth considering that larger sizes, that is, trim sizes larger than 6" x 9" or 7" x 10" may pose a problem for some book stores.

Many book shelves won't easily handle books bigger than that. Unless you're producing an art book, you probably don't want to end up with a book that won't fit anyone's bookshelves.

If at all possible, pick an "industry standard" size. Which means, give careful consideration to the standard trim size of 6 x 9 inches.

Use Styles For Formatting

You will want to start each chapter of your book on a new page. You will probably want to use different fonts for headings, sub headings, footnotes or to draw emphasis.

Would you like to skip a line after each paragraph or would you like for a certain font to automatically be used after each special title. You can accomplish this and more using styles.

An added benefit to using styles is that should you decide to publish an eBook version of your manuscript, you will be happy that you used styles to perform the majority of your formatting, since that method of formatting is more compatible with eBook conversion protocols..

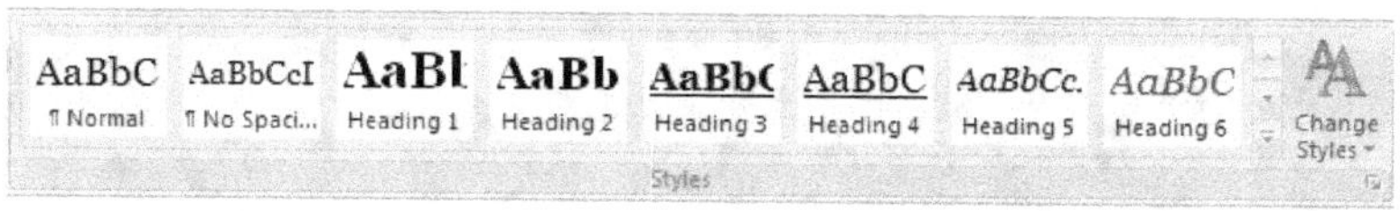

figure 1A: Styles menu in Microsoft Word

The style menu is located within the home tab of Word. Right click on one of the styles, in the resulting drop down menu and click 'Modify.'

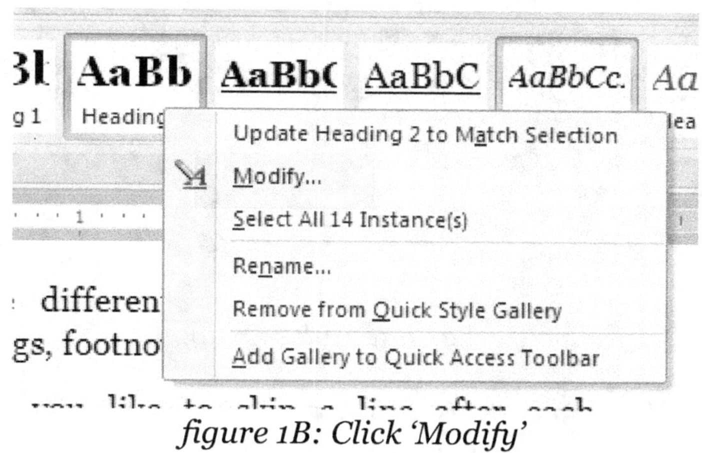

figure 1B: Click 'Modify'

Clicking modify here opens the style formatting dialogue box where you can select font, text color, level of indent, line spacing after and various other formatting options for that particular style.

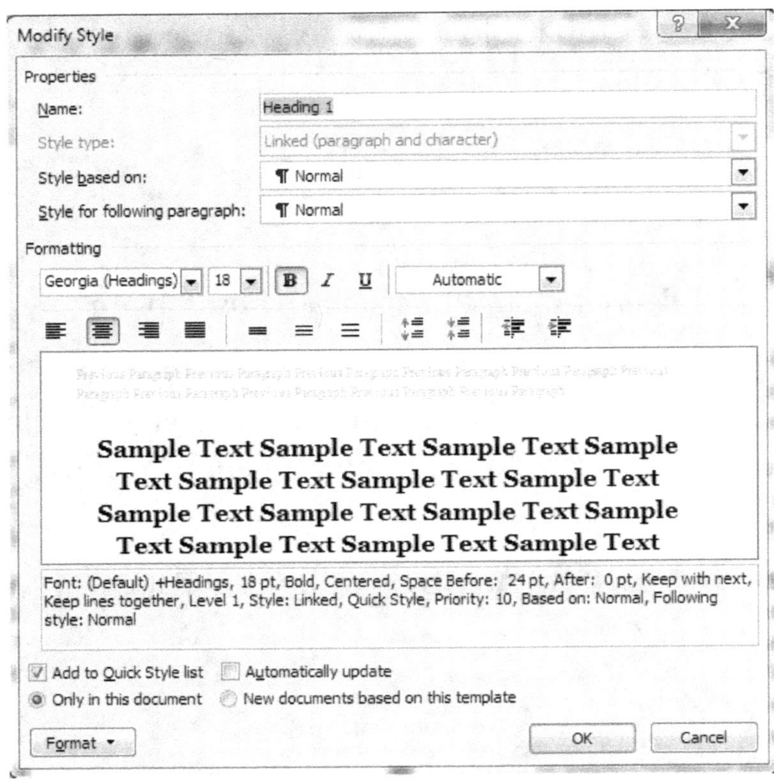

figure 1C: Format Styles Dialogue Box

Another great advantage of using styles for formatting a print version of your manuscript is that by using styles for the first several levels of headings, you can automatically create a table of contents.

Note: The table of contents generated in this manner has no practical use for eBook formatting and would need to be removed prior to conversion.

The instructions above assume that you are using Microsoft Word as your writing and editing platform. If you have chosen to use one of the other platforms such as:

- Scrivener:
  https://amzn.to/2LqSort
- Google Docs:
  https://www.google.com/docs/about/
- Freedom:
  https://freedom.to/
- Ulysses (Mac):
  https://ulysses.app/

Be sure to check that respective application's instructions for working with *styles* and other formatting conventions.

READY, SET WRITE

Now that you have decided on the physical characteristics of your book, it is time to actually write your book.

There is however, at least one more crucial decision left to make. Which writing platform will you use to write your book?

Choosing a Writing Platform

We have all seen cartoons where a caveman chisels messages onto stone tablets using a hammer a chisel. We have also all seen TV shows and movies where a writer types a ream of pages and proudly presents the stack of papers to his or her significant other as *'the manuscript.'* You may have also seen images of a writer actually committing his or her creative musings, for publication, using nothing more than pen and paper.

Today, those romantic images are nothing more than just that; romantic images. Writers today use a variety of electronic devices that center around a computer.

While the product of writing may still be referred to as a manuscript, the part of that word that indicates a manual process is not as accurate as it may have been in days gone by.

<u>Voice to Text Software</u>
Also known as Speech to Text software. Voice to text refers to the practice of converting the spoken word to actual text just as if those words were 'typed.'

This process may be as simple as recording information using a voice recording device. Then later playing that recorded information back so that it can then be manually typed, thus converting voice to text.

There is also technology available that can take spoken words and convert them directly into text.

One of the leading software products that can reliably take your spoken words and convert them into text and boasts an accuracy level of over 99% is *Dragon Naturally Speaking,' by Nuance.*

- https://amzn.to/2zZjfVH

There is a feature of some versions of _Dragon Naturally Speaking_ that allows you to record material onto a hand held device then later connect that device to your PC. The software _listens_ to your pre-recorded material and converts it into text.

- https://amzn.to/2LuL3FR

Choosing the *Write* Medium

When you start to actually write your book's content, you will be faced with the choice of which medium or software application to use.

There is absolutely no shame in using your favorite word processor. This book was written entirely using Microsoft Word 2007.

If you are just getting started as a writer, sticking to the word processor that you are familiar with has its advantages.

- You avoid the distractions caused by having to learn how to use a new software package

- Your work will tend to flow more smoothly because you can focus on your content and not on your software

- You also save money because you didn't have to purchase additional software.

Of course, there may be disadvantages to using your word processor, as well.

- A word processor may limit your ability to organize and structure your book

- You may need to be able to look at research while in the process of writing

- You may require tools such as a spell checker, thesaurus, and/or grammar checker that your word processor may lack

- Your content may require you to manage graphic images and charts

- You may desire to include footnotes and indices

Your word processor may provide limited conventions for handling all of these features and more, however, your word processor may likely lack the many robust options for handling such features as can be found in some of the more popular writing applications that are used by professional book writers.

With a typical word processor, you may not be able to 'see' the book in its entirety, nor be able to move easily between different sections or chapters.

While this is not meant to discourage you from using your favorite word processor, many successful writers manage to do well with the likes of Microsoft Word or Word Perfect, the intent here is purely to make you aware of options that are available.

Should you decide to go with a writing software package, choosing the best one for you can be a daunting task.

Choosing a Writing Software Package

Different writers need different tools, and it all depends on the format and features of his or her book, as well as, his or her writing style, and on his or her personal preferences.

The following is a brief description of six of the best writing software packages on the market:

<u>**Scrivener**</u>:
<u>by Literature and Latte $45</u>
Perhaps the most popular among professional book writers who prefer book writing software.

Scrivener helps you organize your work. You can set word count targets, and you can also output a print-ready version of your book.

The software program is available for download at Amazon.

You can buy a Mac version, or a Windows version and it has a free trial. Click below to download a free trial:

- https://amzn.to/2OaKvU3

Using the standard '*corkboard*-and-*index-cards*,' approach to organization, Scrivener works exactly the way we might plan a book on paper.

You can break your writing down into manageable chunks without losing the thread. Where it comes out on top is chapter sidebar and outline screen that allow you to always keep a visual tab on the development of your book, and add in notes and ideas on the fly.

The main disadvantage of Scrivener is that it comes with a bit of a learning curve, and you can't do the spell and grammar checks that you can in Word.

yWriter5:
by SpaceJock Software; (free to download)

- http://www.spacejock.com/yWriter5.html

If Scrivener looks a little daunting, then yWriter may be an easier place to start. It's free, which is always good which means that if you're not sure that you even want or need writing software, then it's a good place to start

Although designed with the novelist in mind, nonfiction authors will also find it easy to use and fit for purpose.

yWriter5's main attraction is its simplicity. It doesn't come with fancy 'extras' to distract you from your writing.

Second to its simplicity is the way it keeps your work organized. This is important because a book may become too big to see and edit in a single document.

yWriter5 breaks your writing into chapters and then further into workable chunk sized scenes or sections for nonfiction writers. It keeps a tab on where everything is.

The focus on scenes or sections is a very manageable way to write.

yWriter5 has easy-to-use navigational tabs so the writer can move between chapters and there are no hidden secrets that take time to learn.

Simple, functional, and it does what is advertized.

The storyboard function is nice for novelists, and nonfiction writers may enjoy being able to see the visual flow of their book.

In conclusion, yWriter5 is perfect for the writer who likes no-frills organization and is less concerned about the look of their software.

yWriter5 is only available for Windows, at the time of this writing.

For collaborative projects, smaller and more frequent work, and easy marketing, Fast Pencil's Book Writer is a well-developed application that is easy to use and comes with different advantages to the other software packages.

Firstly, you can automatically update to your FaceBook page or Twitter timeline whenever you start or finish a new project. This is good marketing because you are seeding the idea of your book as you go. You keep your followers updated on your progress and generate engagement with your process, especially if you are also blogging about your book.

The Book Writer editing software is easy to use, and there are plenty of helpful 'how-to' videos if you get lost.

One of the main selling points of *Book Writer* is the collaborative nature of it. You can share your work with other writers, as well as beta readers, editors, or publishers. This includes service providers you might work with to self-publish. Your collaborators can log-in from any device as long as there is an internet connection.

For editing and tracking changes, *Book Writer* incorporates an auto-edit tracking system.

The main disadvantages of Book Writer are the added cost of formatting and publishing through them. The price jumps from $9.99 to access the writing software, to $675 to publish your manuscript, at the time of writing. And, with Fast Pencil, as soon as you decide to format your book outside of their templates, costs mount.

With few exceptions, there will be costs involved however you decide to publish, but at least know what you are in for before you decide to go this or any other route.

Especially when comparing Fast Pencil with, say, Scrivener, which can export your manuscript in many publishing, formats at no additional cost.

This software requires that you be logged onto the internet in order to use it, though it works for both PC's and Mac's.

The collaborative nature of this software will be just perfect for some projects, but if you don't need that particular feature, then *Fast Pencil Book Writer* may not be a reasonable choice for your writing.

<u>Ommwriter:</u>
<u>by Herraizsoto & Co, minimum $4.11:</u>
- <u>https://ommwriter.com/</u>

The Writer's Haven. Or so it says in the marketing material.

It's basically a text editor, but what makes it unique amongst the writing software packages is the addition of music and a calming, and simple, environment. Right on your desktop.

The developers charge a fee based on what the user wants to pay starting at a minimum of $4.11. If you want to pay more, the developer only asks that your offer end with the numeral '1.'

You download the package to your computer. You can then choose from 7 meditative tracks carefully chosen to keep your focus, and a selection of relaxing colored backgrounds.

When you press save your work is saved as either an 'omm' file or you can choose to save your work as a text file.

If you like the sound of tapping keys you can also turn on keyboard sound.

The background designs are referred to as chromatherapy which are designed to make the screen easier on the eye and to complement the mood you are creating.

The main drawback of *Ommwriter* that you can only write and then export a text file.

All the formatting will have to be done either in a publishing software package such as Sigil or a more sophisticated tool such as Scrivener.

Noisli

by Noisli, Ltd. :

- https://www.noisli.com/

One of the great features of Noisli is that it has a timer.

It's very similar to Ommwriter, except that you have to be online to use it. This can be a major disadvantage if you want to work sans an internet connection.

Otherwise, it is simple to log-in through your web browser, create an account and just write.

You can download your work as a text file to your computer or to Dropbox (which is nice if you're working on a tablet for example). And you can set a timer.

Sigil

By Strahinja Marković, free to download:

- https://sigil-eBook.com/

If you plan to publish an eBook Sigil is a strong option for both complete beginners and those of you who are more advanced in the art of coding eBooks.

Sigil is a free, open-source software program for making eBooks that can make either simple or more complicated formatting for a digital book. If you want to format your own books, then you'll appreciate *Sigil*.

With a book browser, a document viewer and table of contents all on the same page, the layout is intuitive and is easy to learn.

It has a WYSIWYG editor (what you see is what you get), so you see how your book looks before you export.

You can import a HTML file and Sigil will tidy it up and erase any errors in the script, and it also allows for inserting images and graphs throughout the book (which is often a tricky part of formatting an eBook).

It also has options for chapter breaks and it spell checks.

If your book is uncomplicated and easy to structure and layout, don't shy away from using Sigil to help you do it.

When you're thinking about how to write a book, you need to realize that no writing software, no matter how perfect, can actually write the book for you, but it's definitely worth finding one that can help you along the way.

Don't get caught up in deciding between all of the options, as with writing, it's better to just start. Choose a medium and take a test drive. Start with something simple and then you can progress to a more advanced or sophisticated platform when you've mastered the ins and outs of writing software.

The Content _IS_ the Book

Now that you have considered all of the options available, before you commit to building your book's content it's time to sit down and write.

You may have notes gathered in no particular order on little scraps of paper including ketchup stained napkins.

You may have only an idea and a strong desire to put those ideas in writing. You realize and are intrigued by the fact that once published, your book and in some ways, your name becomes immortal.

There is no right or wrong way to start writing a book. The important thing is that you get started. And as Wallace 'Famous' Amos once said, "Do something, do it now and do it every day."

Writing With an Outline

If you were to toss out the word "outline" to a room full of writers, you might just start a small riot. The feeling about outlines would range from, "I hate them" to "I always start with an outline."

It is wrong to assume that an outline will stifle your creativity by holding you to some rigid set of ideas. After all, it is your outline just as it is your book.

You have the ability to alter your outline even to the extent of discarding it and starting over.

For the fiction writer an outline can help you flesh out your most promising story ideas, avoid dead-end plot twists and pursue proper structure. It can save you time and prevent frustration.

For the nonfiction writer, an outline can be an invaluable aid. It can help you to organize the chronology of the information that you intend to present. It can also serve as the map for your research efforts.

For the nonfiction writer, an, outline provides an instant checklist for those items that need to be covered.

Whether you are writing a fiction or nonfiction book, an outline can be your best friend. It can help you to organize your thoughts which will then be reflected in the organization of your book.

How To Best Use An Outline
To get the most out of the outlining process, you would begin with the development of your premise and work all the way through to a complete list of scenes or points of information.

Keep in mind that there is no right or wrong way to outline a book. The only requirement is that you find the method that works for you. If you start outlining and begin to feel the technique isn't working for you, rather than denouncing the outline process entirely, adjust the process and the outline to better suit your personality and creative style.

For The Fiction Writer
- Craft your premise. Your premise is the basic idea for your story

- Roughly sketch scene ideas. Armed with a solid premise, you can now begin sketching your ideas for your story

- Create your characters. Who are they? What is their relevance to the story?

- Interview your characters. Get to know their backgrounds

- Explore your settings. Discover details about your surroundings

- Write your complete outline. Make your outline summarize your story

- Put your outline into action. Expand your outline into your complete story by filling in details

For The Nonfiction Writer

- Construct an outline based on the major points

- Arrange the major points in the order that you intend to present them

- These major points become chapter headings

- For each major point, add minor supporting points. Add as many minor points as necessary to expound on and illuminate its major point

- Using the outline as a guide, fill in the detail that completes your new nonfiction book.

Writing Without an Outline

Of course, it is possible to write an excellent book, fiction or nonfiction, without the use of an outline. Many writers choose to do so.

For the fiction writer, start with the main character. He or she has a goal. This goal is the center of their existence. Almost everything they do centers around the fulfillment of that goal. Then add something or someone that interferes with their achieving that goal. Build your story and all of the significant characters and locations from there.

For the nonfiction writer, start with the end. What is the book about in summary?

Once you have summarized your book, tell your readers how you arrived at that conclusion. If the summary describes the tastiest blueberry muffins on earth, now tell us what ingredients go into it. Tell us how to pick the best blueberries. Be sure to caution us not to use white sugar instead of dark brown sugar.

These guidelines may or may not apply specifically to what you are writing but the technique will work in a very high percentage of cases.

Formatting As You Go

Now that you are actually writing the book, it is time to put into play those decisions that you may have made prior to actually working on the content of your book.

While it may have seemed strange to consider fonts and right facing page layout versus left facing page layout before you started to write, if you did those things - made those decisions, now is the time that those decisions will start to pay off.

You will find it so much easier to format your book as you write it rather than have to go back after it is finished.

If you format as you go, when you are finished, you will be glad that you did.

The Writer's Toolbox

There are a handful of tools that you may find helpful as you write. And just like a mechanic's or a carpenter's toolbox, there are tools that you may never use, that you may use once or twice and then there are the tools that seem to never leave your hand. The rule is:

"It's better to have it and not need it than to need it and not have it."

Here are a few tools that you might find useful, feel free to add your own favorites:

Dictionary

Either a hard copy or an online version will help you get at the true meaning of words as well as the correct spelling.

- Dictionary by Merriam-Webster: https://www.merriam-webster.com/

<u>Thesaurus</u>
A thesaurus comes in handy when you search for a word or maybe you have a word but you would rather use a different word with the same or similar meaning. You may prefer the big book or the online version, either way, a thesaurus can be a valuable tool for a writer.

- Thesaurus by Merriam-Webster: <u>https://www.merriam-webster.com/thesaurus</u>

<u>Grammar & Style Guides such as:</u>
- <u>The Elements of Style</u> by Strunk and White <u>https://amzn.to/2KBd9zT</u>

or...

- <u>The Tools of the Writer</u> by Roy Peter Clark <u>https://amzn.to/2KBcRsN</u>

<u>Urban Dictionary (online)</u>
The Urban Dictionary is a crowd sourced online dictionary for slang words and phrases.

It can be invaluable when writing dialect or if you need to translate dialect.

- https://www.urbandictionary.com/

<u>Google</u>

Google is a primary research tool for many writers, and the first place to start rooting around for data to give a story context and credibility

All data is not created equal, of course. So try to seek out primary and reputable sources. Such as:

- Major media outlets (NY Times, Washington Post)
- Government agencies
- Original research reports
- Well-known experts
- Authoritative nongovernment agencies (Pew Research, for one)

Beware search responses have the '*Ad*' indicator. These responders pay Google a fee in order to appear at the top of your search results. They may or may not lead to the accurate information you seek.

Figure 2 - Google Ad

Bitly

If you are planning to include URL's (the internet address of a web site) in your book, Bitly and be a valuable tool. This is especially true if you are planning to publish an eBook.

Bitly can convert a long URL such as:

https://www.publishersweekly.com/pw/by-topic/authors/pw-select/article/61059-pw-select-february-2014-which-eBook-publisher-is-right-for-you.html

to the much shorter and more manageable:

https://bit.ly/2ur3fGN.

Both of these URL's will take you to the same web site. Try it! It's FREE!

Bitly also offers several other resources such as the ability to brand, track and optimize your URLS's.

- https://bitly.com/

A NoteBook

To jot down your thoughts. Not just those thoughts that pertain to your book.

A writer writes.

The more you write the better and more comfortable you will become at expressing your thoughts.

A Voice recorder

Use it just as you would a noteBook. You might look into acquiring a speech to text software package such as Dragon Naturally Speaking.

- .https://amzn.to/2zZKkbd

Google Docs
More than letters and words, Google Docs brings your documents to life with smart editing and styling tools to help you easily format text and paragraphs. Choose from hundreds of fonts, add links, images, and drawings. All for free.

- https://www.google.com/docs/about

Speech to Text Software
This powerful tool allows you to talk to your computer and have the computer type what you say to it. There is even a feature that allows you to use a hand held recording device when you are away from your computer, then later connect the device to your computer and have it listen to your recorded voice and type what you recorded.

The most popular speech to text software is Dragon Naturally Speaking ($29.80):

- https://amzn.to/2IYlism

With the voice recorder option ($67.95):

- https://amzn.to/2tZyDfl

<u>A book</u>
Any book.

Writers are readers.

Preferably a book that relates to what you are writing about. But by all means read. Whenever you are not writing and you are able, read.

Take note of the author's writing style. Especially if you are particularly fond of an author. Take note of what it is about this writer's style that touches you.

Ask yourself; "How can you develop a style that may touch your readers?"

Staying Motivated – Fighting Writer's Block

Sooner or later it happens to every writer. Your mind is blank, you feel totally disconnected from your story. Your conscience may even rebel against you and tell you that you are wasting your time.

Sounds like you have a case of Writer's Block.

Writer's block takes many forms and it can be triggered by many events, such as, but not limited to:

- a disappointing outcome of something you were depending on
- a soured relationship
- a noisy environment
- bringing the workplace home
- money problems
- friends and/or family request or demands
- loneliness

- doubting that you really want to expose yourself publicly by writing
- fear of rejection
- boredom

Let's face it, it may prove to be difficult to sit at your computer and just write. Especially when there are so many other things pulling at you. So many other feeling and emotions that are creating distractions that prevent you from concentration. Telling you to stop writing.

When that happens, that is exactly what you should do"

Stop!

If you are unable to focus, the quality of your writing will be seriously affected, and that is not what you want; to write junk. The best thing you can do at this time is get away from your writing, for a while.

Here are a few suggested activities that may help you shake your writers block:

<u>Realize that this is temporary and will pass</u>
Many times emotions are related to certain hormones and chemical balances (or imbalances) within the highly complex

machinery of the human body. What we eat, even what we ingest in the air, affects how we deal with relationships, information, conversations and any other external stimulus.

In other words, that extra slice of pizza may heighten the tension between you and your brother-in-law and negatively affect the way you feel about writing. But only temporarily.

Like most all emotional crises, the intensity tends to subside as time passes,

<u>Go for a walk</u>
Get out of the house, explore nature. Recall just how beautiful life is. Notice the beauty of a young couple holding hands, or children playing or birds singing. Recharge your spirit by taking in your surroundings.

<u>Eliminate distractions</u>
Turn off the TV, the stereo; send the kids out of the room or even out of the house. You may have to remove yourself from the distractions if you are unable to eliminate them. In that case go to the library or to the park. Go to a friend's` house. Go somewhere where you are able to concentrate in peace.

<u>Do something to let off some steam</u>
This method is especially effective if your writer's block is caused by frustration or anger. Try running or punching a heavy bag. Swimming is also a good way to burn off negative feelings that are blocking your creativity. Anything that you can do to work up a sweat and get your heart rate up will ultimately help you to relax and it is easier to focus when you are relaxed.

<u>Play</u>
Play a game of chess or monopoly. Play your favorite video game. Computer solitaire is a personal favorite. Play with a child or children. But by all means play. Playing has a way of relaxing the mind and establishing a somewhat carefree state over ones entire mindset.

<u>Change your environment</u>
Distractions are not the only reason to venture away from your desk. A trip to the library will expose you to people who are about some endeavor that may or may not be creative. The fact is that whatever the others are involved in, the atmosphere is one where people are attempting to focus and concentrate. Can you

think of other environments that may be conducive to your creative effort?

<u>Read a book.</u>
Writer's read. I find that when I read, it makes me want to write. When you hold a book in your hand, realize that at some point another person was where you are and that whatever it was that may have hampered their success, they were able to overcome. Open the book and spend some time visiting that person's creation and surely you will find the inspiration to get back to work.

<u>Freewrite</u>
Write about anything, fiction or nonfiction. This writing has nothing to do with your book. This writing is more about venting or letting you emotions express themselves. This writing is like punching the heavy bag so let it all hang out. Just be careful that something you write may be offensive to someone else so after you Freewrite, be sure to shred, burn or otherwise destroy your *'work.'*

<u>Let the music play</u>
Preferably instrumental music because lyrics may be distracting in that they may tend to send your mind wandering down memory

lane. With that in mind, you might want to avoid music that may tend to bring back memories, music that you are very familiar with. If at all possible, select music that you have not heard before.

<u>Spend time with someone who makes you feel good</u>
Do you know someone who always makes you laugh? A favorite aunt or uncle, an old college roommate? Someone who is always glad to see you? A visit with an elderly person can lift your spirits and get you back in front of your computer.

More than anything, realize that whatever is distracting you from writing is only temporary. Don't give up. Believe that you can do it.

If *I* can do it...

What's in a Title

Your title should be:

<u>Easy to Say</u>

If your title is difficult to pronounce, it may cause potential readers to not connect with your book and purchase another title instead. People would also be less likely to recommend your book if they can't pronounce the title.

And, if you spend a lot of time correcting media and potential readers, you could appear awkward and possibly unyielding.

<u>Short and Sweet</u>

Short titles fit in URLs, tweets and most anywhere you need to use them, plus they are easier to type and say. Short titles will also be easier to read in eBook stores on digital devices, which have very small display spaces and screens. Try to stick to about five words or less. If you need more words to provide needed context, consider adding a subtitle.

<u>Easy to Remember</u>

An important form of the publicity for your book will be word of mouth. Make sure your title is memorable so that potential readers can remember it when they look it up or purchase it later.

Descriptive

Your book title should include keywords that describe the most important thing, person or idea in your story and demonstrate its significance.

Easy to Repeat

You are going to say, type and read the name of your book over and over, thousands of times. Make sure it is something that you can be comfortable saying repeatedly. Think of how easy it is to say your name repeatedly.

Project Your Book's Genre

The title of your book should give potential readers a clear indication of your book's genre. You don't want your mystery to sound like a self-help or comedy book.

Funny (where appropriate)

If appropriate for your book's genre, giving your title a humorous twist can make it more memorable and attract more readers.

<u>A Preview</u>
Your title should give a hint of your story, but not give everything away. Leaving something unanswered will motivate potential readers to purchase your book.

<u>Complement the Cover</u>
And vice versa. Your title and cover should work together to enhance the shelf appeal of your book. The effective coordination of title and cover design will draw the potential reader in and perhaps stimulate the all important purchase of your book

Judging a Book by its Cover Design

Creating your book cover should come only after you've picked the title for your book. If you haven't yet picked your title, stop. You must decide on a title before you start designing your cover because your title and cover must work together.

Once you've determined your title, and only then, can you move on to designing your book cover.

Your book cover sends a message. Regardless of the quality of the art work or whether there is no artwork at all, your book cover sends a message. Whether the message sent by your book cover is effective at stimulating interest in your book and ultimately the purchase of your book depends on several factors that you can control.

In general, nonfiction speaks to the brain while fiction speaks to the heart. Novel book covers do great when they send an emotional message relevant to the story. Nonfiction book covers that are witty and intriguing sell well.

When you select your title, you should have a clear idea of what message you want your book cover to send.

<u>No Need to Re-invent the Wheel</u>
Take a stroll through your nearby Barnes & Noble, Books A Million or other 'brick & mortar' book store.

I recommend going to an actual bookstore rather than browsing online booksellers such as Amazon or The Book Depository so that you are able to touch and feel the actual books. You will also be able to envision the true scale of the artwork and not be limited to thumbnail images.

While your most productive observations will come from books in the same genre as your book, don't hesitate to borrow ideas from books of other genres that may have clever titles.

In addition to finding a book cover design that you may want to loosely replicate, you are also looking to be inspired.

If You Design Your Book Cover Yourself
There are many tools to choose from should you decide to tackle the job of designing your book's cover yourself.

There are many online tools that will guide you through the graphical aspects of book cover design at no cost. There are others that charge a fee that varies from modest to proud.

The difficulty in the use of these tools also varies greatly. There are those that require little to no previous experience in graphic design as well as those that require expert level experience.

Here are a few recommendations:

- Canva: https://www.canva.com/

- DIY Book Covers: http://diybookcovers.com/

- The Creative Penn: http://thecreativepenn.com

Canva

Canva is a **Free** design tool that you can use that offers tons of book cover templates for just about anything you'd want to design, including book covers for each genre. It's very easy to use, but also somewhat limited in what you can create.

DIY Book Covers

DIY Book Covers allows you to design your own cover with **Free** templates and tutorials based on the principles that work for bestselling books. It's a tool, a guide and a template system all in one.

<u>The Creative Penn</u>

Is the brainchild of Joanna Penn. Joanna Penn helps authors make a living writing through her bestselling books, courses and podcast. Her website offers tools for aspiring writers to help them design their own cover. In addition, the site offers tools to help you write publish and market your book.

If You Decide to Seek Help With Your Book Cover Design

Almost without exception, you will be required to pay a fee for professional help with designing your book cover. Depending on the finished result, the cost may be well worth the price.

Here are a few recommendations:

- EBook Launch: https://eBooklaunch.com
- Damonza: https://damonza.com
- 100 Covers: http://100covers.com
- Reedsy: https://reedsy.com
- 99 Designs: https://99designs.com

EBook Launch
Professional quality book covers at an affordable price.

Damonza
Professional cover design team with hundreds of books under their belt.

100 Covers
A very affordable option ($100 in most cases) for those who need a professional cover design.

Reedsy
A marketplace for vetted book designers with high accomplishments in the industry. You're sure to find a cover designer or interior designer with experience in your genre here.

99 Designs
You create a virtual design contest by telling them what you're looking for, and you'll get lots of options in return. At the end of the week, you get to pick your favorite design. If you don't like any of the designs at the end, you get your money back. You can even get design help for other parts of your *author brand* here too, such as logos and business cards.

<u>Book Cover Graphics and Images</u>

Should you decide to go it alone (or almost alone) you may be interested in obtaining images from the web. Just as in the case with cover design, there are free graphic images as well as those you have to pay for.

Here are a few resources for free images:

- Flickr: https://www.flickr.com/creativecommons
- Pixabay: https://pixabay.com
- Pexels: https://www.pexels.com
- Free Images: https://www.freeimages.com
- Unsplash: https://unsplash.com

And, of course, here are a few sites that charge a fee for you to use their book cover art work:

- Depositphotos: https://depositphotos.com
- Stock unlimited: https://www.stockunlimited.com
- Shutterstock: https://www.shutterstock.com

Illustration

Many of the same resources listed above for cover design may well serve your purposes for internal illustrations.

If you are writing a children's book, the illustrations are critical, perhaps more so than for other types of books.

You may be writing a book with technical specifications that require very detailed illustrations.

You have two basic options:

1. Do the illustrations yourself
2. Have someone else do the illustrations

If you are capable of creating the artwork for your book you are in business, however, if you are not so endowed. Even if you have the skills, you may have no desire to take on the responsibility. In that case it is fortunate for you that there are qualified artists available who will gladly illustrate your book. Of course, expect there to be a fee involved.

There is a variety of organizations from which to mount your search for an illustrator.

<u>The Society of Children's Book Authors and Illustrators</u>
A wonderful place to start (and consider joining) is the Society of Children's Book Authors and Illustrators.

This is a member based creative organization and it possesses a wealth of information on publishing such as industry tips, directories, artist portfolio's and contact information.

- https://www.scbwi.org/

<u>Childrensillustrators.com</u>
Another source is Childrensillustrators.com, which is primarily a portfolio directory site. It is a visual playground for creative talent sorted by medium, style and subject. If you are unfamiliar with the artistic style you want – reviewing portfolios will give you a better understanding to your preference.

- http://childrensillustrators.com/

<u>Google</u>
Don't forget the power of a good Google search. Most professional illustrators have both a blog and website, which gives you a more intimate look at the creative person behind the art.

How Many And What Type Illustrations Do You Need?

You must decide how many and what type of illustrations you will employ in your book. If you are writing a picture book, decide between full page spreads or single page art. If you are writing a book for young adults, perhaps one illustration per chapter will suffice.

Set A Realistic Budget For The Project

It is possible, though highly unlikely that you will find a professional illustrator who is willing to do your book for free, for their portfolio or for a split of future royalties. Though this is not unheard of, this situation is extremely rare.

When you approach an experienced professional illustrator with a query, you should do so respectfully and be prepared to pay them for their time, effort, talent and experience.

The going rate for an illustrator of children's picture books (based on a 32pg book) estimates range from $3,000 – $12,000, plus royalties. Another way to look at it is, if you estimate that an illustrator is creating 20 original illustrations for your book and you are paying them $3,000 for art that is $150 per illustration. Now consider how much time goes into each illustration, starting with thumbnail sketches, revisions, pencil outlines and final color. Oh, and don't forget the cost of supplies, along with the artist's time.

Proof Reading

Proofreading performs a vital role. Proofreading is the process of correcting surface errors in writing, such as grammatical, spelling, punctuation and other language mistakes.

You might be comfortable calling on a friend or family member to take on the job of eliminating mistakes and inconsistencies in your manuscript however, make sure that friend or family member is up to the task. .

Bear in mind that a professional editor is a far more accomplished proofreader than your typical friend or family member and any computer program that Google has even dreamed about.

A professional editor understands the conventions of English writing and the nuances of the language. He or she is trained to be methodical, and through experience can identify and eliminate common errors.

A professional editor can catch easy to overlook mistakes; he or she is experienced in identifying inconsistent terminology, spelling and formatting.

Proofreading is an important service because any writing intended for publication, whether an academic article, book or business document, must communicate its message in the clearest possible way.

For writing to be clear, there must be no spelling, grammar or punctuation errors. There must be no inconsistency in language.

Such errors will certainly undermine the impact of your writing as well as diminish the credibility of you, the author.

Proofreading For Yourself

You may opt to proofread your book yourself. If you do, you have the option of just digging in starting from the first page or you can take advantage of tools and guides that are available online.

Many *self proofreaders* will proofread a book with software that allows them to mark errors on a PDF formatted manuscript.

Self-publishing authors often do the same, using these two free software options:

- PDF XChange Editor – by Tracker Software: https://www.tracker-software.com

- Adobe Reader XI - by Adobe: https://acrobatusers.com/assets/

Both applications have drawing tools and text tools that allow you to circle errors, insert missing words, and make notes in the margins without disrupting the book designer's layout. You can even mark errors with proofreading stamps.

Both of these options work with PDF formatted files in order to not alter page layout and other structures that have been built into your book.

There are many web sites that are designed with the aspiring author in mind. These web sites offer tips and guides. They often alert you to some of the common mistakes and errors that writers at all levels of experience may be prone to make.

Here are some of the web sites that may prove to be helpful, should you decide to proofread your book yourself:

- 7 Tips for Proofreading Your Book – The Book Designer: https://www.theBookdesigner.com/2015/08/7-tips-for-proofreading-your-book/

- 10 Proofreading Tips For Self-Publishers - by MEDIASHIFT: http://mediashift.org/2013/02/10-proofreading-tips-for-self-publishers-058/

- Proofreading Tips and Tools for New Writers - by Become a Better Write Today (Brenda Berg): https://becomeawritertoday.com/proofreading-tips/

Editing

What's the difference between proofreading and editing?

If you diligently proofread your book, why then would it need to be edited?

The difference between proofreading and editing is simply this:

Proofreading will correct errors in spelling, grammar, syntax, punctuation, formatting and word usage (such as its or it's). Therefore, proofreading normally takes place at the end of the writing process as a final step.

Conversely, editing takes a deeper look at how information and ideas are presented. While editing includes all steps involved in proofreading, the focus of editing is making changes that make your book easier to understand, better organized, and more suitable for the audience.

Editing for Yourself

As with proofreading, you have the option of enlisting the services of a professional editor or taking on the task yourself.

And as with proofreading, should you decide to take on the task yourself, there are several web sites that offer tools and tips to get you on your way to becoming an *'edited,'* published author.

Here are some of the most popular websites that offer tools and tips to help you edit your book:

- Self-Editing Basics: 10 Simple Ways to Edit Your Own Book - by The Write Life: https://thewritelife.com/self-editing-basics/

- How to Edit Your Book In 4 Steps - by Writer's Digest: http://www.writersdigest.com/editor-blogs/

- How to self-edit your book (25 writing tips for indie authors) by Creativindie: http://www.creativindie.com/

To Proofread, Edit or Both

Now that you are familiar with the differences between book proofreading and book editing, it is entirely up to you to make an informed decision on which of the two or both will best serve your needs. After all, it is *your* book, so it is *your* decision.

It is also your decision whether to take on the task of proofreading and or editing yourself or to seek professional help with either or both.

Seeking Professional Proofreaders and or Editors

There are several web sites that are created both by the professionals themselves as well as organizations where the members are the actual professionals.

Here are a few of the organizations with whom you may consult to find professional help

- GlobalEnglishEditing by Global English Editing: https://geediting.com/

- Proofreading & Editing Services For Hire Online by Fiverr: http://www.fiverr.com

- Book Editing by Professionals - Fast and Available 24/7 by Scribendi: http://www.scribendi.com/book-editing

- Professional Book Editing Services For Independent Authors by Standout Books Publishing Services: https://www.standoutbooks.com/

How to Get Published

There are two principal ways that books are published.

There is also a third which I highly recommend for the first time author. That method is a combination of the first two principals.

Your choices to get your book published are as follows:

1. Traditional Publishing
2. Self Publishing
3. A combination of the two

First, let us define the first two, *principal* methods by which books are published.

Traditional Publishing

Traditional book publishing is when a publisher offers the author a contract and, in turn, prints, publishes, and sells his or her book through booksellers and other retailers.

Traditional publishing is the best way to get your book onto the shelves of brick and mortar book stores.

The publisher essentially buys the right to publish your book and pays you royalties from the sales.

In order to publish a book traditionally, most writers need to find an agent. In order to find an agent, you must identify the right category for your writing. If you are or want to be a nonfiction writer, you will need to submit a book proposal with three sample chapters, and a synopsis of each chapter. If you are writing fiction, you must have your manuscript complete.

Once you a ready to find an agent, do your research. Check out websites such as:

- WritersMarket.com: http://www.writersmarket.com/

- Writer's Digest Magazine: http://www.writersdigest.com/

The Literary Agent Query Letter

Once you have done your homework, you're ready to write a query letter. This letter is what you will send to potential agents.

It's important that the query letter is made up of the required parts:

- the synopsis of your book
- the chapter summary
- the market or audience for whom your book is meant
- a description of yourself.

There is no standard format for a query letter that all writers subscribe to. Just bear in mind that a query letter is a business document and, accordingly, it should look like a one page business document.

Your query letter should be limited to 300 – 400 words max. Since many agents will browse queries using their phone or tablet, it is important that your letter be organized such that it looks well on a small screen.

Keep it concise, orderly and well organized.

"Dear Ms. Brooks"

Is a perfectly fine way to start your letter, of course, assuming that the agent's name is Brooks and that she is, indeed, a woman.

The following line should then make the agent prick up their ears.

"I'm writing to seek representation for my 89,752-word debut thriller, The Candy Cane Killer."

The title, genre, and word count: three key pieces of information are right there in your first sentence. With that out of the way, let's really grab their attention!

Researching the Agent Shows You Did Your Homework

"According to your agency's website you're actively seeking middle-grade fiction, so I'm pleased to introduce my novel."

<u>Setting The Hook</u>
Within the first few pages of a book, fiction or nonfiction, you need to make it impossible for readers to put your book down. In a query letter, you have to do the same with just a few lines. This part of the letter is known as the "hook."

Your hook should show agents how your book is different from the thousands of others in its genre.

It could be an awesome concept that makes the reader wonder why someone hasn't thought of it before.

"About Marylyn, there were three things I was absolutely positive. First, she was a murderer. Second, she liked it— and I didn't know just how strong her drive to kill might be — how intensely she longed to spill my blood. And third, I was unconditionally and irrevocably in love with her."

Not only does this introduce the genre and tone (dark, sadomasochistic romance), it sets up the narrator's dilemma; he knows he's in love with a woman who might kill him. What will happen next? Is he walking into a trap? Will his love conquer the killer's thirst for blood?

<u>The Tantalizing Synopsis</u>
Now that you've "hooked" the agent, it's time to reel them in with your synopsis and get them to request your manuscript.

"The synopsis should serve to get an agent interested in your book, though you are not attempting to tell them everything about your book.

Your synopsis is your opportunity to introduce:

- The plot (fiction)
- The primary characters (fiction or nonfiction)
- The central questions or conflicts that drive your story (fiction or nonfiction)
- The benefits of reading this book (nonfiction)

Your synopsis should then tantalize, draw the agent in and piqué his or her curiosity.

Look at what other authors wrote on the back cover of their books:

A synopsis.

Think about this as if you're writing the back cover of your own book.

The following is an excerpt from an actual and I might add, successful, Literary Agent Query Letter:

Dear Ms. Collins:

I am writing because I'm currently looking for an agent to represent my novel.

Let me tell you a little about myself: (Here you would put in your own biographical information).

The novel that I've just finished is a love story, told in third person, from the point of view of a woman named Finny Short.

It begins when the main character is fifteen, and it moves across twenty years of her life, ending when she's thirty-five. In addition to being a love story, it's a story about a young woman embarking upon the adventures of growing up.

Adventures in which she meets many lively and eccentric characters, including a seductive heiress named Judith Turngate, a domineering-but-kindhearted mother figure named Poplan with a love of exotic Asian fruits and Irish fiddle music, and a narcoleptic piano teacher named Menalcus Henckel whose mysterious past turns out to bear on Finny's future.

My aim was for the book to be a densely plotted Dickensian adventure in which a young person emerges into the world. But instead of having it be a young man, such as David Copperfield or Augie March or T.S. Garp, I wanted to write a World According to Garp about a woman, navigating the hilarious and treacherous and heartbreaking paths of adult life.

I have enclosed an S.A.S.E. for reply, or you can contact me by email or phone – whatever's best. I would love to send you the novel, if you think this book might be of interest to you.

Thanks so much for your time.

All best,

Justin Kramon

Courtesy Writer's Digest: Guide to Literary Agents; copyright © 2018

Getting published the traditional way is hard, but it is not impossible.

You may be rejected by the first or subsequent literary agents, just don't give up. There is always the option of self-publishing.

Self Publishing

One way to guarantee that your book will be published is to publish it yourself.

Self publishing describes all types of publishing in which the author assumes the majority of, if not all of, the financial risk.

Self publishing comes in many forms. Here is a brief description of the major types of publishers and/or self-publishers.

- Print On Demand (POD) Publishing
- Vanity Publishing
- Subsidy Publishing

Print On Demand (POD) Publishing

POD stands for print-on-demand. POD publishers can print your book at a moment's notice—as few as two or as many as 2,000 or more. POD publishers are generally independent publishers or self-publishing companies.

Some POD Publishers are:

- Instant Publishers:
  https://www.instantpublisher.com/

- IngramSpark:
  https://www.ingramspark.com/

- Outskirts Press:
  https://outskirtspress.com/selfpublishing

Vanity Publisher

A "vanity" publisher prints books at the author's expense. The author is responsible for paying the publisher's profit and overhead costs. These publishers print anything for anyone who can pay their fees. They may offer marketing help, warehousing, editing, or promotion of some sort.

(CAUTION: the term "vanity publisher" is considered pejorative and outdated by many in the larger publishing industry; use it carefully or not at all.)

For that reason I have elected not to list any so called vanity publishers.

Subsidy Publisher

A subsidy publisher shares the cost of (or subsidizes) publishing a book. Subsidy publishers are often selective, and the completed books belong to the publisher, NOT the author. The books remain in the publisher's possession until they are sold, but authors collect royalties. Though at first glance they may seem similar, subsidy publishers are NOT generally considered to be traditional publishers.

Some publishers who publish some or all of their books on a subsidy basis are:

- Ink Water Publishers:
  https://inkwater.com/

- Blue Dragon Publishing:
  http://blue-dragon-publishing.com/

- AuthorHouse:
  https://www.authorhouse.com/

The term self-publishing can refer to several types of publishing. What they all share in common is that the author absorbs some or all of the cost of publication.

Historically, the term self-publisher refers to an author who starts his or her own publishing company or one who pays ALL costs of printing and is responsible for marketing, distribution, promotion, etc.

Today that is rarely the case. Many of the publishers that cater to the self publisher offer such services as proofreading, editing, illustrating, page layout, cover design, marketing, distribution, promotion, etc. a la carte.

This flexibility in choosing services from the publisher allows the author more control over many aspects of his or her book from production to distribution and sales.

From Self Published to Bestseller

There are many books that went on to become bestsellers, though they started off among the ranks of the self published.

A few of those books are:

"Eragon," is a young adult fantasy series written by Christopher Paolini, who began writing it at the age of 15.

- https://amzn.to/2LGpyin

"The Joy of Cooking," was privately published in 1931 by Irma S. Rombauer, a homemaker in St. Louis, Missouri.

- https://amzn.to/2LwKnjt

"Rich Dad Poor Dad," is a financial advice book written by American businessman, author and investor Robert Kiyosaki.

- https://amzn.to/2LFnXcs

"No Thanks," is a 1935 collection of poetry by one of America's most famous poets, E.E. Cummings. After being rejected by publishers, Cummings self-published the collection with the help of his mother.

- https://amzn.to/2zZ65Ia

"Remembrance of Times Past," an epic novel by Marcel Proust has been called "the most respected novel of the twentieth century."

- https://amzn.to/2NCFowu

"The Tale of Peter Rabbit," was originally self-published by Beatrix Potter in 1901. After receiving rejection letters from publishers for a story she had made up to entertain a sick boy, Potter, a 35-year-old writer and illustrator, took matters into her own hands and printed 250 copies of the book.

- https://amzn.to/2NwAory

"Your Erroneous Zones," by Wayne Dyer who originally self-published his self-help book with a print run of 4,500 copies.

- https://amzn.to/2uGAKoR

"What Color Is Your Parachute?," a job-hunting guide by Richard N. Bolles, has been on the New York Times best-seller list periodically for more than a decade.

- https://amzn.to/2NCE30o

"The Celestine Prophecy," was self-published by James Redfield after being repeatedly rejected by publishers.

He sold 100,000 copies of the novel out of the trunk of his Honda before Warner Books agreed to publish it.

- https://amzn.to/2O6jJfD

After 10 years of rejections, Michael J. Sullivan quit writing altogether. Then, one day, he sat down and wrote *"The Riyria Revelation"* fantasy series. He still couldn't find a publisher, so Sullivan self-published through Ridan Publishing, a company started by his wife.

His sales were so impressive that he re-solicited mainstream publishers, and this time received several offers.

"The Riyria Revelations" has now been translated into fourteen languages. In 2012 io9 named him one of the "Most Successful Self-Published Sci-Fi and Fantasy Authors."

- https://amzn.to/2LFgDO5

BE ENCOURAGED!

<u>Famous Authors Who Self Published</u>

Tom Clancy's first novel, *"The Hunt for Red October,"* was acquired by the Naval Institute Press in Annapolis, Md., when an editor there, Deborah Grosvenor, became enthralled by Clancy's novel, convinced she had a potential bestseller in her hands.

The rest is history as Tom Clancy has published at least 12 books.

Clancy is just one of an unbelievable roster of authors whose names are household names to today and share in common the fact that at one time they self published their work.

Such writers as:

- Edgar Allan Poe
- Mark Twain
- L. Frank Baum
- Stephen King
- William Strunk Jr.
- John Grisham
- Jack Canfield
- Beatrix Potter

For those having difficulty breaking into print, self-publishing has long been a suitable alternative. However, some self-published authors do much more than get by. Self-publishing has proven to give many writers a jumping off point in an eventually illustrious career.
Some writers actual make their living (and quite a living) as self-published authors.

The Third Way To Get Publish – Self Publish Then Pursue Traditional Publishing

This method of getting published employs both self publishing and traditional publishing.

The advantage of this method is that you realize a return on your investment of time and money much sooner than you would if you depended exclusively on traditional publishing.

To get a book published via the traditional route can take years.

With self-publishing, you can have your book in your hands in a matter of days. This is especially true if you self-publish through Amazon's Kindle Direct Publishing (KDP).

Get your book in your hands by whatever self publishing means fits your particular situation. Once your book is in print, you can become a selling, marketing, promoting machine at the same time that you are seeking a literary agent through a carefully crafted query letter.

As a published author, you are also able to seek speaking engagements.

Speaking engagements can potentially net you a speaking fee as well as the potentially lucrative back of the room sales.

eBooks

What is an eBook?

Even the term eBook (as it is used herein) tends to vary in form. Some refer to them as an eBook or an eBook or even an epub or an e-pub or an ibook, to name a few. In general, all of these terms refer to the same thing.

An eBook is a book that is read on an electronic device (computer screen, tablet, Smartphone or e-reader). An eBook differs from an epub, a word document or a PDF file.

While it is possible to read your friend's news article or your neighbor's recipe book on your Smartphone, it does not count as an eBook if you can change the text. eBooks made for public distribution are in a format that is almost impossible to change.

EBook reading apps are designed to restrict any kind of editing while leaving open the possibility of adding notes and highlighting without changing the original file

While a PDF format document may be literally impossible to edit, PDF documents still do not qualify as eBooks.

You cannot change the layout while reading a PDF file on an e-reader device. A PDF is the ideal format for a document that is to be printed. It is designed with the exact paper size in mind. It always looks like the print version. It never changes.

eBooks, on the other hand, are created in a format that changes shape according to the device you read it on. The chapters and paragraphs do not change, but the line breaks aren't forced. It will always perfectly fill your screen.

We have come to expect websites to change their layouts whether we are looking at them from our tablet or phone; the same goes for eBooks.

With an eBook, URL's are likely to be *hot*. Meaning that if you click on it, your web browser will attempt to pull that URL up.

Locations indicated in a page of contents or index may also be hot, in that clicking on a referenced location within the document will take you to that new location. There may also be other hot objects that may bring up images, definitions, bibliographies and more.

How (and Why) To Publish an eBook

eBooks are far more profitable for the author than printed books. There is much more profit per eBook because there is no printing, warehousing, storage or shipping.

Readers can also buy immediately; as soon as they hear about your book.

You may publish only a print version of your book, but you stand to risk losing considerable revenue from eBook sales.

You can sell your eBooks to anyone in the world over the internet without printing or shipping costs. With eBook publishing, you really can have a multinational global business from your writing desk, which is very exciting!

It is better to publish a print version as well as an eBook version. Bear in mind that many successful authors publish exclusively in the eBook format.

As with hard copy publishing, you have the option of having a publishing company convert your manuscript to eBook format and distribute it or you can do it yourself.

3rd Party eBook Publishing

Many publishing companies offer to publish either a hard copy version of your book or an eBook version, or both.

These companies boast design teams who are well-versed in eBook conversion for distribution on all prevailing platforms. There are 3 principal platforms for eBooks:

- Amazon *Kindle*
- Barnes & Noble *Nook*
- Apple *iBooks*

If you're looking to publish only in *digital*, you will want to employ the same high-quality design and editorial expertise as you would with a physical book.

Choosing a Publishing Company for Your eBook

When choosing a publishing company for your eBook it is always important to <u>*read the fine print*</u> to determine which service is right for your book, and your budget.

Many publishing companies offer add-on options with costs approaching upwards of $1000 or more. These options might promise publicity or editorial support.

You may only be looking for a cheap and quick way to get your book to the masses.

You may be seeking a service that lets you add audio or high-resolution photographs to your book

Whatever your individual needs, there is very likely an appropriate eBook publishing service, and often more than not, one that can and will accommodate you.

The following is a summary of some of the more popular companies. To find more I suggest you visit the very insightful web article on the Publisher's Weekly web site; *"Which EBook Publisher Is Right for You?"*:

- https://bit.ly/2ur3fGN

As an alternative to the above web site or in the event that the site or page is no longer available, Google *"eBook publishers."*

Mascot Books - (Print & eBooks):
A full-service publisher, Mascot has the tools, the team, and the experience to help authors at any stage in their process.

With an emphasis on a flexible production schedule that fits your needs of the author.

- https://mascotbooks.com/

Rakuten kobo; Kobo Writing Life - (Print & eBooks):
Kobo Writing Life offers a user-friendly, five-step process for uploading manuscripts. The company will convert your manuscript into an e-pub file for free, with no additional cost to the author.

- https://www.kobo.com/us/en/p/ writinglife

Blurb Books - (Print & eBooks):
Blurb Books places an emphasis on its print book options, but also offers fixed format eBooks, which are sold through the Blurb Bookstore and Apple's *iBookstore*. Blurb charges a one-time $9.99 eBook publishing fee.

While more limited in discoverability than other platforms, Blurb is ideal for authors who have a design-heavy project like a cookbook or children's book. Authors can also create enhanced eBooks with audio and video.

- http://www.blurb.com/

BookBaby - (Printing & eBooks):
BookBaby offers global distribution to the major eBook retailers including Amazon, Kobo, Nook, and iBookstore. With three publishing packages to choose from, authors can supply their own e-pub file for free or opt to pay $99 for the conversion. Royalties are 85% of net for the free and standard packages and 100% of net with the premium package ($249).

- https://www.bookbaby.com/

Depending on the service selected, the author may have to do more or less of the actual formatting and other tasks themselves.

The responsibilities placed on the writer in order to publish an eBook through an eBook publishing company may be similar to the responsibilities of the writer who self-publishes his or her own eBook.

The fact is that eBook publishing is a very technical field which, like the World Wide Web itself is evolving rapidly. Whatever the tasks delegated to the author in order to get an eBook published may only scratch the surface of those tasks that are performed by the publishing company.

That is a major consideration when choosing an eBook publisher. You must weigh what you ultimately want in your finished eBook against how much of this will be done by the publisher, how much must be done by you and how much this all will cost.

So I will end this section with the advice with which I started it:

Read the fine print.

Self-Publishing Your eBook

Just as the world wide web speaks various forms of HTML in order to display and reconcile its interactive content, so the world of eBooks speaks its own languages.

Depending on the platform your eBook is to be published to, your manuscript will have to be converted to one of several formats.

Some of the eBook formats that are widely used are as follows.

Mobi

The eBook format used by the MobiPocket Reader. MOBI was originally made as a PalmDOC format's extension. It can be opened using MobiPocket's reading software, which can be installed on a lot of PDAs and Smartphone's.

Third party readers such as Stanza, FBReader, Kindle for PC and Mac, and STDU Viewer can open MOBI files.

Epub

The ePub format is an open format designed by the Open eBook Forum and developed by the International Digital Publishing Forum.

Software that can opened with this format are the ePubReader, Firefox add on, Adobe Digital Editions, and QuickReader.

Devices that can open this file format include the iPhone, iPod, iPod Touch, iPad, Sony Readers, Kobo Reader, and the Nook from Barnes & Noble.

AZW

This is an Amazon eBook format used exclusively on the Amazon Kindle. It is basically a MOBI format that uses a high compression option.

Kindle apps have been released for devices other than the Kindle reader, AZW format files can now also be opened on Smartphones (iPhone, Android, and BlackBerry), computers (Mac's and PC's), and tablets (iPad, Android tablets, and Windows 8 tablets).

LIT

This is an eBook format developed for the Microsoft Reader software. It is native to the PocketPC and Windows Mobile devices, and can also be found on PCs and the Hanlin eReader.

Please note that content in LIT format was discontinued starting November 2011, while downloading of the Microsoft Reader software was stopped by the end of August 2012. Users may still use the Microsoft Reader on their devices but can no longer add new content.

ODF

ODF stands for Open Document Format. It is an XML-based file format and is the default format for OpenOffice, an open source productivity suite that is becoming a popular alternative to Microsoft Office.

IBA

An IBA file is an Apple iBooks Author eBook format. iBooks Author (iBA) is a free eBook authoring application by Apple Inc.

PDF

The PDF format is not a true eBook file format. It is included here because of its widespread popularity as a portable file format.

The Portable Document Format (PDF) was created by Adobe for its Acrobat products.

This is a very popular file format since software support for this format exists for a wide variety of devices.

Examples of PDF viewers are Adobe Reader, Foxit Reader, Nitro PDF reader, PDF-XChange Viewer, Xpdf, and a lot more. Most of these software packages are freeware.

One downside to this format is that content in PDF is usually scaled for A4 or letter size, which becomes unreadable when reduced in order to fit the small screens on Smartphones. The PDF format is most suitable for print applications.

Converting Your Manuscript For eBook Publication

There are several excellent eBook writing and conversion apps available with prices ranging from free to hundreds of dollars and they are available for every platform.

Many writers use Microsoft Word, Scrivener or another word processor, then take upon themselves the task of converting their manuscript into eBook format only to realize many hours into the project that it might not be as easy as they have imagined.

If you are at the point in the writing process where you are investigating the publication of an eBook from your completed manuscript, you may well come to appreciate that at the beginning of this book, while exploring how to write a book, I discussed the format essentials of book publishing long before any discussions on book content. And if you heeded said advice, this is one of the key places where that advice pays off.

Text editors and eBook converters might look similar on the outside, but they have very different purposes.

Word processors help users to work with the text; write it, edit it, share it with your editors, betas, and grandmother. Word processors have built-in spell check, most of them follow user changes and support different note-taking and highlight options.

eBook editors, on the other hand, come into the picture once your book is ready: they are designed to create an epub, Mobi, AZW or other format file that is difficult to impossible to change by the user.

These files display according to the publisher's intents on many different devices, whether it be a computer, a Kindle or a Smartphone.

Most eBook reader apps and devices allow the user to change the font size, font type, line space and even the background color, or disable these qualities altogether. Most of these devices and apps offer a standard, one-size-fits-all design.

The bottom line is, whatever formatting you use, will likely be overwritten by the user. This means that there is no need to spend hours selecting the perfect color of your headings; it is possible that only a percentage of your readers will ever see it.

This does not mean that you should not use any formatting or that there is no need to expend the effort to create a beautiful epub, quite the contrary.

There is one thing that you certainly need in order to create a beautiful epub, and that thing is *consistency*.

Make sure that whatever formatting you use is consistent throughout your book. If one of your paragraphs has a double line spacing and 12pt font size, the next should not be 11pt only to be able to fit it on the same page.

When creating a long document, it is easy to forget what your previous chapter title looked like or whether you used block quotes or an indent of 1" or 1.5".

Editing Your Manuscript For eBook Conversion

If you intend to publish both a print version as well as an eBook version of your book, the following instruction is critical.

Because as you prepare your manuscript for conversion, you will make changes to it such that it will hardly resemble the manuscript that will ultimately become the print version of your book,

The solution is to make a copy of your manuscript which will be edited for eBook conversion. One copy will retain all of the formation that you so wisely included because you heeded the advice given earlier in this book.

From this point forward we will address the copy only.

Remove All Formatting

For the conversion to work properly and for your book's formatting to be consistent, you will have to format using general styles instead of using local formatting. Styles format texts on the level of a paragraph.

(A paragraph is a text between 2 forced line breaks: your chapter titles are paragraphs as well.)

To start with a clean slate, it is best that you remove all formatting. Although this is a rather drastic modification to your hard work, it is quite necessary.

The following edits can be most easily accomplished using Google Docs.

If you prefer using Microsoft Word or any other writing platform, simply ignore the following instructions.

<u>Introducing Google Docs</u>
Google Docs brings your documents to life with smart editing and styling tools to help you easily format text and paragraphs.

And to top it all off. It's free.

- https://www.google.com/docs/about/

Open your file in Google Docs.

Press CTRL+A to select the entire document, then go to the styles (it should be somewhere at the top) and select Normal.

If you are using Word, follow the above instruction but instead, click the 'Clear All Formatting' button to remove all formatting.

Please note, that this will remove all formatting, including italics and bold. To keep italics and bold, press CTRL+A to select the whole document, then go to the styles, and select Normal. If you have all text selected but your Font and Font size fields are blank, it means that there is still some local formatting left somewhere.

To solve this, just select a simple, common font like Arial or Garamond and 12pt size. This is not the final formatting of your book: you will add the formatting back again later.

<u>Manually Remove the following:</u>
Before you add the formatting back, you must clean the manuscript of the remaining formatting that was not removed by the previous steps. Your task is to remove everything that is unnecessary, such as:

- Automatic numbering

There is an exception with which automatic numbering can work; if your items are immediately one after the other, like this:

1. Item
2. Item
3. item

On the other hand, current epub standards are unable to handle numbered lists if you are "breaking" the list somewhere then trying to continue it.

This happens if you add extra blank lines or extra text between numbered items.

For example, what looks like this on your screen:

```
1. Chapter
Lorem ipsum dolor sit amet, donec quod faucibus
fusce rutrum lacinia dui, auctor viverra,
tristique lacus cras pellentesque, curabitur
faucibus.

2. Chapter
Mi vestibulum sed. Scelerisque aliquam lacinia,
quis rutrum tincidunt aptent bibendum nostra
justo.
```

figure 2A: Auto Numbering Before

Will most likely look like this on the eBook reader:

```
        1. Chapter
Lorem ipsum dolor sit amet, donec quod faucibus
fusce rutrum lacinia dui, auctor viverra,
tristique lacus cras pellentesque, curabitur
faucibus.

        1. Chapter
Mi vestibulum sed. Scelerisque aliquam lacinia,
quis rutrum tincidunt aptent bibendum nostra
justo.
```

figure 2B: Auto Numbering After

To switch off automatic numbering, select all of the numbered text, click the little numbers sign.

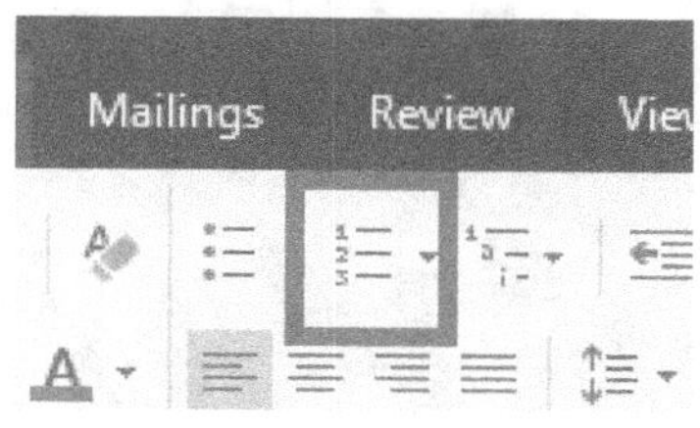

figure 3: Automatic Numbering Button

You'll then have to enter your numbers manually. If your book contains many instances of automatic numbering be sure to go through and manually convert them all to "real" numbers.

- Page numbers

Remove page numbers from the footers and/or headings. To do so in Word, double click the top or bottom of the page to open the Headers and Footers menu, and click Remove Page Numbers.

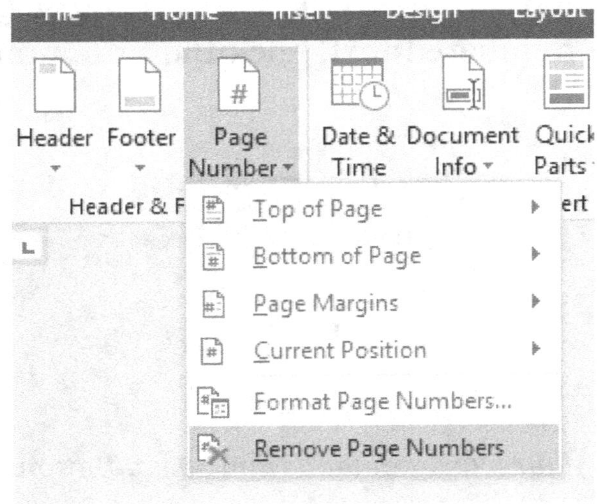

figure 4: Remove Page Numbers

Be sure to also delete any references to page numbers (e.g., if you say something like: see it on page 20, instead say something like see it in Chapter 1). You can easily do so by pressing CTRL+F and search for the word "page."

- Remove the Table of Contents

While every book should have a Table of Contents, the one you insert at the beginning of your document, won't work.

It either loses its ability to be clickable, or it keeps the page numbers: page numbering does not make any sense when it comes to an eBook.

Therefore, we need to remove the Table of Contents.

To remove your Table of Contents, click References, then select Table of Contents on the left, and click Remove at the bottom.

You will create a Table of Contents that is compatible with epub during the actual conversion.

- Forced line breaks

You may have used soft or hard line breaks to solve the problem of orphans and widows, if so there is work to do.

Select the little paragraph icon (¶) on the Home tab in Word to show all non-printing characters. This will display all "invisible" formatting signs. Your text will look somewhat like this:

Lorem·ipsum·dolor·sit·amet,·consectetur·adipiscing·elit.¶

Cras·fringilla,·eros·in·consequat·↵
sollicitudin,·eros·lectus·iaculis·dui,·sed·lacinia·↵
elit·leo·in·tellus.·Aenean·↵
aliquet·viverra·convallis.·¶

Aliquam·quis·fringilla···nisl,·non·ullamcorper·↵
nisl.·Quisque·laoreet,·dui·facilisis·dictum·iaculis,·¶

figure 5: Displaying Hidden Characters

You will see a ¶ for every hard break (paragraph break) and a ↵ (soft return) sign for every soft line break. The little dots stand for space.

Make sure that you only have paragraph breaks ¶ at the end of paragraphs, and nowhere else.

If you see any paragraph break or soft return that should not be there, simply delete it.

- Double spaces

Go to Find and replace and replace all your accidental double spaces with one space.

To do so, press CTRL+H, and press the Space twice ( ) in the Find field. Then go to the Replace field, and press the space only one time ( ).

- Double paragraph breaks

Do not manually add extra breaks between paragraphs. At the end of the paragraph, it is enough to hit Return only once; if you need some space between the paragraphs, we can add that later using styles. If you are signaling a substantial break within a chapter, please insert one line with three asterisks, like on the following example:

Lorem ipsum dolor sit amet, consectetur adipiscing elit, sed do eiusmod tempor incididunt ut labore et dolore magna aliqua.

***

Ut enim ad minim veniam, quis nostrud exercitation ullamco laboris nisi ut aliquip ex ea commodo consequat.

Start each chapters on a new page.

While it is common to start a chapter on a new page, do not add more paragraph breaks to make something go to the next page.

Use CTRL+Return to insert a page break before chapters to get your chapters to start on the next blank page. You can also use the Insert Page Break function.

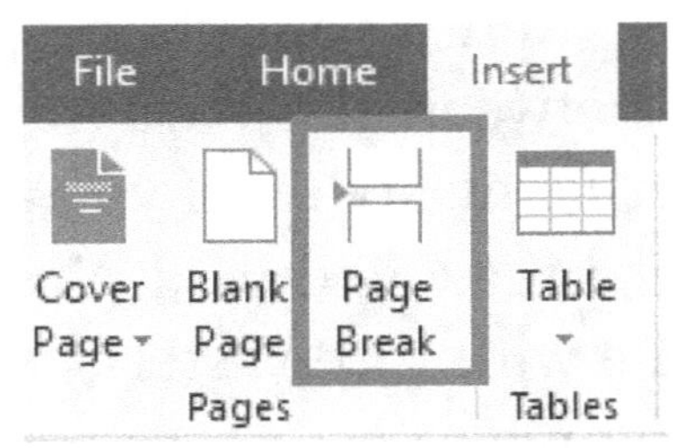

figure 6: Insert Page Break

- Remove All Tabs

Do not use tabs for aligning paragraphs. Remove them all for now. You will add indents later. Press the ¶ sign to show all hidden characters.

A little arrow stands for tabulators, like on the picture below:

> →   Vestibulum tortor libero, iaculis nec diam vitae, ultrici
> blandit non malesuada ut, placerat vel sapien. In gravida so
> ipsum. Nam sed malesuada risus. Fusce sodales sollicitudin l
> Donec a tortor leo. Pellentesque dolor mi, iaculis in ullamcorper
> erat. Donec id mi blandit, maximus sem ut, congue tellus. Vivam
> ut, lacinia tellus. Phasellus bibendum elit magna, id blandit tort

figure 7: Remove All Tabs

- Image wrapping

Images are best inserted between two paragraphs on a separate line. Do not use image wrapping, turn it off. To set this in Word, click on your image, click Layout Options in the top right corner, and select In Line With Text.

<u>Now Put It All Back Using Styles</u>
Now that you have cleaned your manuscript of all of the little traps that can make your eBook conversion crash, you are now ready to put all of your desired formatting back using *'Styles.'*

Depending on what application you are using, the way that styles will be administered may differ, therefore it is my recommendation that you familiarize yourself with the use of styles for that particular software.

<u>Adding Your Front Matter And End Matter</u>
Your book manuscript is now formatted properly. Your eBook cannot begin with the first chapter, you need a cover, a title page, a copyright page, and a table of contents. At the end of the book, you may consider adding an Author bio and an *other books by you* section.

You are now ready to convert. Just follow the instructions provided by whatever conversion platform you chose to use.

eBook Converters
The following are a few of the top rated eBook converters. Examine a few of them and make your choice based on the platform that best serves your needs.

Calibre

Calibre is a powerful and easy to use eBook manager. Users say it's outstanding and a must-have. It'll allow you to do nearly everything and it takes things a step beyond normal eBook software. It's also completely free and open source and great for both casual users and computer experts.

- https://calibre-eBook.com/

Epubor

Epubor is a great eBook Manager for you to manage your eBooks from different sources. It supports you to classify, modify, convert and transfer your manuscript.

- https://www.epubor.com/

Zamzar

Zamzar is an online file converter, created by brothers Mike and Chris Whyley in England.

It allows you to convert your manuscript without downloading a software tool, and it supports over 1,000 different conversion types. It is also possible to send a manuscript for conversion by emailing it to Zamzar.

- https://www.zamzar.com/

Hamster

Hamster eBook Converter is a 100% free download and an easy way to move eBooks between devices. It allows you to convert eBook files in proprietary formats for Sony, iRiver, Amazon, Kobo, and other eBook readers into a version that can be read on any other reader, or on all of them as a simple PDF or in a file format that they all can understand.

- http://www.hamstersoft.com/free
  -eBook-converter/

ConvertFiles.com

ConvertFiles.com is very powerful file converter that can fit almost all your needs in converting your manuscript into eBook format.

At this point ConvertFiles.com supports 457 possible file conversions and the company is adding more formats and combinations.

- http://www.convertfiles.com/

Amazon Kindle Direct Publishing (KDP)

Amazon Kindle Direct Publishing or KDP as it has come to be know by those who are familiar with it, stands in a class all its own.

Amazon's KDP, in addition to publishing print versions of your book, lets authors convert and distribute their eBooks across all Kindle devices and Kindle apps for free.

Amazon offers two eBook royalty rates: 35% of list price in all territories or 70% of list price minus delivery costs in set territories (and 35% of list outside those territories)

The 70% royalty option comes with pricing restrictions: books must be priced between $2.99 and $9.99 to qualify for the higher royalty rate.

Authors can make changes to their book at any time, and the publishing process is one of the quickest available, with books appearing on Amazon within 24 hours.

<u>KDP Select</u>

KDP Select (kdp.amazon.com/select) allows authors to opt in to a 90-day exclusive digital distribution deal with Amazon in exchange for a few perks. These include KDP Select making authors' eBooks available in the Kindle Owners' Lending Library, where Amazon Prime members can check out their books for free with no due dates. Authors earn royalties on every book that is borrowed.

The program also offers authors the choice between two promotional features: Kindle Countdown Deals or free book promotion. Authors are also eligible for 70% royalty for sales to customers in Japan, India, Brazil, and Mexico.

The big catch to all of these benefits is that while enrolled in KDP Select (90 days), authors must agree to distribute their eBook exclusively through Amazon.

<u>Kindle Unlimited</u>

Kindle Unlimited is a subscription program for readers that allows them to read as many books as they want. The Kindle Owners' Lending Library is a collection of books that Amazon Prime members who own a Kindle can choose one book from each month with no due dates.

When you enroll in KDP Select, your books are automatically included in both programs. Your books will still be available for anyone to buy in the Kindle Store, and you'll continue to earn royalties from those sales.

KDP Toolbox

The KDP web site boasts several tools that help to make this platform for eBook self publishing the cream of the crop. All of these tools work for PC or Mac.

<u>Kindle Create</u>

Use Kindle Create to transform your completed manuscript into a beautiful Kindle eBook. The tool makes creating an active table of contents easy by automatically detecting and styling chapter titles.

It works with several word processing applications (e.g., Microsoft Word, Apple Pages, and Google Docs) that can export to .doc(x) format.

Kindle Previewer

Kindle Previewer is a tool that lets you see how your eBook could be viewed on different devices and screen sizes. This view gives you an idea about the reading experience customers will have on tablets, smart phones, and E-readers of different sizes.

Kindle Textbook Creator

Kindle Textbook Creator is a downloadable tool that helps you convert a PDF of your manuscript, with rich media, for Kindle devices and apps. Kindle Textbook Creator helps you edit materials such as textbooks, cookbooks, travel books, and other titles with rich media such these, to name a few:

- Charts
- Graphs
- Equations
- Audio
- Video
- Image pop-ups

- Inline audio files
- Invisible overlaid audio play buttons

Kindle Textbook Creator is intended for eBooks only. The tool exports the finished eBook to a Kindle Package Format (.kpf) file, which isn't supported for paperback publishing.

Readers of your eBook can automatically take advantage of highlighting, noteBook, flash cards, dictionary look-up and more. Download the tool and, starting with a PDF of your textbook, you can follow the steps in the *Kindle Textbook Creator User Guide* to convert your book for publishing to Kindle.

eBooks created with this tool will work on:

- Fire tablets
- Kindle for PC
- Kindle for Mac
- Kindle for iPhone, iPad, & iPod touch
- Kindle for Android
- Kindle for Samsung

Kindle eBooks with Enhanced Typesetting work the same across devices on various platforms, and they adapt to the changing screen sizes. Kindle Previewer is compatible with *Bookerly*, Amazon's Kindle-exclusive font, and allows you to preview interactive textbook features such as audio and video.

Kindle Kids' Book Creator
Kindle Kids' Book Creator is a downloadable tool that helps you create illustrated children's books. You can import a file from PDF, JPG, TIFF, PNG, or PPM formats. eBooks created with this tool will work on:

- Fire HD
- Fire HD 8.9"
- Fire
- Kindle for iPad app
- Kindle for iPhone app
- Kindle Android app

Note: Kindle Kids' Book Creator and Kindle Comic Creator are intended for eBooks only.

The tool exports the finished book to a Kindle Format 8 (KF8) .mobi file, which isn't supported for paperback publishing.

Also, you'll only be able to create illustrated Japanese-language books with horizontal text in the Kindle Kids' Book Creator.

To create a Japanese-language book, select "English" as your book language and enter horizontal Japanese text for your book content.

Kindle Kids' Book Creator features:

- Features unique to Kindle devices and apps like text pop-ups (for illustrated children's books).

- Add pages and text to imported PDF files.

- Create books with file sizes of up to 650 MB.

- Import illustrations in any of the following file formats: jpg, png, and tiff. You can also import and convert PDF files.

- Use the app in multiple languages, including English, German, Spanish, French, Italian, and Portuguese. Keep in mind that the tool's information page is only available in English, but the app is available in multiple languages.

- Preview how your books look on various Kindle devices before publishing.

Kindle Comic Creator

Kindle Comic Creator is a downloadable tool that helps you create graphic novels, comics and manga (Japanese style comic such as Yu Gi Oh). This tool is recommended for anyone who wants to create Kindle Comics, graphic novels and manga out of their existing artwork.

This tool supports import from PDF, JPG, TIFF, PNG and PPM formats. There is an available instructional video and other resources that are highly recommended before using this tool.

Kindle Comic Creator is intended for eBooks only. The tool exports your finished book to a KF8 .mobi file, which is not supported for paperback publishing.

Documentation for Kindle Comic Creator is available for download in PDF format.

Using Amazon's Kindle Direct Publishing Platform is quick and easy. There is lots of support and there have been volumes of books written that offer tips and strategies for taking advantage of this powerful resource that is advantageous for the novice as well as the experienced writer.

How to Get Paid

Writing for a living offers a ton of advantages; you get to choose when and where you work, and with whom.

No wonder this promise of creative and personal freedom attracts so many people.

Unfortunately, just as many would be writers get frustrated and discouraged. They give up before they reach their goal of making a living as a successful writer.

 So what if you are not a New York Times bestselling author, so what if you don't as yet have a publicist, so what if your Amazon sales numbers are anemic. That is no reason for you to abandon your dreams.

There are techniques that you can employ on your own so that you can start selling your book and even become a best-selling author!

Regardless of what kind of book you've written, or even if your book is still in the planning stages, there are many ways to reach your audience.

Many of the strategies recommended below will cost you nothing at all, others will cost you very little. Choose the one or more that you feel may work for you, master it then choose another. The more of these strategies you employ, the better your chances of seeing a big return.

Begin by perfecting the practice of selling your books *one at a time*. It is only natural to want to sell your book to faceless thousands. Instead, find one person who needs and wants your book. Offer your book to that person.

Then do it again and again and again!

That is the foundation of becoming a bestselling author. Whether you find one person a day, an hour or a minute, your focus is the selling of one book at a time.

<u>It Is Never Too Soon To Start</u>
Ironically, some of the most effective techniques that you can employ in order to increase sales of your book take place before and perhaps *long* before your book is actually written.

One, two or even three years before your book is published, you can and should start building a network of supporters, promoters and reviewers.

Build a database of everyone you meet as you research and write the book. Get their names and contact information, especially their email addresses. Make a note of what you talked about, what their interests are and how you plan to approach them once your book is finished.

Pay special attention to, and make notes about, those who demonstrate a genuine enthusiasm for you and your book.

As your book takes shape, keep in touch with these people. You might send them an occasional email, birthday or anniversary card (electronic cards are free but no less appreciated). You can also keep in touch via a social networking site like LinkedIn or FaceBook.

Include these people as you observe and celebrate significant milestones such as:

- the signing of your book contract
- the completion of the manuscript
- the arrival of the galley proofs
- the arrival of the finished books

You might bring the most influential and enthusiastic, most supportive people from your data base together for an informal gathering. At the *party*, you should be sure to read short excerpts from your book and answer questions.

<u>Participate in and Contribute to Web Forums</u>
No matter what the subject matter of your book, easily nonfiction, but the same can be said of fiction creations; there is a forum or organization that exists composed of people interested in that subject.

The people who make up these forums are veracious readers of publications that pertain to their interests.

It is in your best interest to join and participate in one or more of these organizations.

Contribute to them freely. Give advice and reach out. Offer to help others.

If you vigorously promote these organizations; it will follow that these organizations will promote you and your book.

<u>Reach Potential Readers Through A Blog</u>
Another step that can take place long before your book is completed and early in the process of researching and thinking about your book, is the creation of a blog.

You should contribute helpful, inspirational, perhaps even humorous information each day.

The addition of any information on issues in your field, which is related to the subjects in your book will help to create a genuinely useful body of knowledge.

Put a link to your blog or website in your signature line. When you have a book contract and/or a book title, add the title to your signature line.

<u>Be As Excited About and Committed to Book Promotion As You Are Towards Book Writing</u>
You are obviously committed to writing your book.

The time and effort that will go into writing (or went into writing if your book is completed) demonstrates your commitment. In order to get paid, and to get paid *big*; you have to develop that same excitement and commitment towards promoting your book.

Think of book promotion as storytelling. The story you are telling is why you wrote your book, how it can help others, and how the world will benefit from your book.

Once you develop a positive attitude about book promotion, people will pick up on it, and tune in to it. Some writers hold the mistaken attitude that says, "I am a writer. Marketing is the publisher's job. Promoting my own book is not my responsibility."

While a writer with that attitude may make some money, or even a good deal of money, they are missing the boat when it comes to the big money.

Remember this; no one can promote a book more effectively than the author.

The truth is; except for writers such as Stephen King, Terry McMillan, James Patterson or Oprah the publisher probably won't expend a great deal of money to market your book.

You must adopt the attitude that; "If I don't promote my book, no one else will."

<u>Employ The Power of a Media Kit</u>
The centerpiece of your media kit are professionally printed business cards with the book cover on one side and your contact information on the other side.

Under no circumstance should you try to print them on your home printer. An investment here in your product as well as yourself will pay off royally in the long run.

That's not all, your media kit will also contain the following items.

A head shot by a professional photographer or a talented amateur. It should be well lit, with a neutral background. Be very aware of the background.

Keep it simple and free of distractions. Something you will not have to be concerned about in a professional photographer's studio.

Look right into the lens and make sure that your eyes are clear and sparkling.

Compose a 100 to 150 word biography. The main purpose of the biography is to tell a reader why you are uniquely qualified to have written this particular book.

Construct what, in the publishing industry, is referred to as a *'one-sheet'* for your book. A one-sheet is a single piece of paper with a glossy print of the book cover on one side and a one-page description of the book on the other side.

Be sure to include a few short comments and recommendations from colleagues and associates in the description. Don't be afraid to drop names (and titles) here.

<u>Compose Sales Pitches</u>
You will need at least three sales pitches for your book. The sales pitches should be 10 seconds, 30 seconds, and 60 seconds in length.

When someone asks what your book is about, give them the 10 second pitch. If the person responds with interest, have a longer pitch ready.

Practice your pitches on friends and family until they are each second nature to you. Practice until you can pitch your book in your sleep.

<u>For Each Book; its Own Website</u>
As publication day approaches, build a full website. The website should feature:

- A book blog, in which you write updates, corrections, errata and respond to reader comments and suggestions. This book blog may become the basis for a second edition of your book.

- Sample chapters from your book

- A link to the Amazon page for your book, so people can buy the book online

- Items from your Media Kit

- Book reviews and comments.

- Your schedule of appearances, including bookstores, speaking engagements and conferences

- Your contact information.

Solicit Book Reviews
Between six and nine months before your book is due to appear on the market, start asking people for reviews and comments.

Send reviewers a printed galley proof of your book. If you don't have printed galley proofs, send a PDF containing the first two chapters, a table of contents and your bio.

It is important that you approach the 'biggest names' in your field. Ask for both reviews and comments. Busy people may only have time to write a few sentences.

Don't be shy; remember if you approach someone who is a published author, they most likely will appreciate your effort because at some point, they were in your shoes.

Write Articles

You should take advantage of opportunities to promote your beliefs, your ideas and, of course, your book. There are several platforms that are available for you to contribute articles, such as:

- eZines
- websites
- magazines

Some of which are sure to advocate or deal with the subject matter of your book.

Find them.

Once you know where they are, look through them and figure out which ones talk to the audience for your book.

Contact those sites or publications and pitch articles that will be of interest to their readers. After all, their readers make up *your* audience.

Schedule articles to appear around the time your book will appear in bookstores and on Amazon.

For example, if your book is going to appear in bookstores and on Amazon in mid-June, schedule your articles to appear in July, August, and September.

Remember to pitch articles early, because many magazines and eZines have a 3-6 month lead time.

Be sure to mention your book title somewhere in the article. In online articles, link the book title to its Amazon page so readers can click over and buy the book.

Become an Amazon Affiliate so that links to your books (as well as millions of other products) earn you additional profits when purchases are made via your affiliated link. For more information on becoming an Amazon Affiliate go to:

- https://affiliate-program.amazon.com/

<u>Solicit Book Reviews from eZines and Magazines</u>

Ask websites, eZines and magazines in your field to review your book. Some websites or eZines may offer to trade, to review your book if you write an article for them.

<u>Collect 20 Reviews on Amazon</u>

Amazon reviews are amazingly effective. Everyone from book buyers to publishers reads them.

Your goal is to get at least 20 reviews. Contact everyone you know and ask each of them if they would give your book an honest review. Let them know it can be brief. If they agree, send them either a galley proof, a promotional copy of the book, or a PDF containing a table of contents, two sample chapters, and your bio.

Amazon's Top Customer Reviewers are another source of high-value reviews. Find the reviewers who deal with books in your area. Write to them. Tell them you have written a book they might be interested in, and that you'd appreciate a review.

If they respond, send them a galley proof, a promotional copy of your book or the standard PDF promo containing a table of contents, two sample chapters, and your bio.

Be Sure to be Mentioned in Email Blasts

Look for organizations in your field that send large-volume emails. Try to get your book reviewed in their email or newsletter by sending your promotional materials to them.

Be a Speaker at Conferences

As a published author, you have the qualifications necessary to speak at conferences. Contact conference organizers at least 6 months in advance.

At first you may have to register or even pay a fee to speak. Later, when you become better known, conferences may seek you out, and may even pay you to speak.

You should be prepared to give a 45 minute presentation. A useful way to structure a 45 minute presentation is to speak for 30 minutes, and take questions from the floor for the last 15 minutes. Plan to take a few minutes after your speech to circulate with the audience.

Have a table in the *back of the room* where you or someone on your team sells your books. Be prepared to sign (autograph) your book.

Be sure to get permission from the hosting organization to sell your books.

<u>Make and Post Online Videos</u>
Make a few 5 minute videos of yourself talking about key issues in your field. Put the book title and URL on the bottom of the video screen and in the credits.

Post your videos on several of the many video sharing sites including sites such as:

- blip.tv
- jumpcut
- ourmedia
- Vimeo
- Social
- YouTube

Embed the video clips on your website.

<u>Be Consistently Persistent</u>
Plan on following your promotional strategies at least an hour a day for at least a year or more. Resolve to do something every day on promotion.

Remember follow-up and persistence are the keys to success.

<u>Writers Are In-Demand Public Speakers</u>

On your way to becoming a bestselling author, realize something that many recording artists have long ago come to accept.

The money from selling records is good, but the money from personal appearances, concerts and the like, is great!

Here are strategies to help you get those potentially lucrative speaking engagements.

<u>Be Willing to Speak for free.</u>
Before you get to be a professional at anything, you need to spend some time as an amateur.

The best way to bridge the gap between being an amateur speaker and becoming a professional speaker is for you to speak a lot, even if it means speaking for free.

Reach out to your local rotary and Lion's clubs, small chambers of commerce and networking groups. That way, you can hone your content and get lots of practice. Plus, as you get better, you can use these places as references for when you're pitching paid gigs.

They may seem difficult to find, but there are myriad events happening in just about every city every single day. Most of these venues have little or no budget at all for a speaker and will be more than happy to have you speak at their event.

Just be sure to bring a carton of your books for the 'back of the room' sales that might take place.

<u>Hone Your Craft As You Go</u>
Speaking for free gets you warmed up, but you must take it seriously.

Your non paying audience may not be very demanding which can lull you into a habit of giving lack luster performances.

Never mind that they may or may not be an enthusiastic audience. Never mind that you may perceive a certain inattentiveness. All of this is an opportunity for you to get good.

Develop the ability to capture your audiences' attention. Make them pinch themselves and wonder, *"How were we able to book this guy or gal for free?"*

In other words, you must be willing to give a $5,000 performance for free.

And when you have honed your craft to that point, you will no longer have to speak for free.

As a professional speaker you are the writer, the director, the actor and the producer of a one person show. Just having expertise in a subject isn't enough anymore. Audiences and meeting planners (the ones who pay the big bucks) expect an extraordinary experience.

No, you will not be expected to sing or dance, but you will be expected to entertain while you educate and inspire them.

Your objective is to become an amazing speaker; to get paid and asked to come back again and again and to be highly recommended.

To be highly recommended you must be highly engaging, highly informative and connect with your audience. Then you can be highly paid.

<u>Add Value to Your Presentation</u>
As you hone your craft and work through your material, concentrate on how you're adding value to your audience. Make sure that they take away something from your talk that they did not have before.

As you transition from a free speaker to paid speaker, focus on that *value* which is indeed what you charge for. If you have a *'formula,'* a 'system' or a 'program,' give it a name, and be specific as to whom it benefits.

<u>Organize Your Marketing Materials</u>
Before anyone will hire you, they want to know how you speak and what you speak about.

Having the right web presence as a writer and speaker helps to get you found when an organization is searching for an expert speaker on a certain subject. Perhaps the subject that you have written about.

Once this organization has found you, they want to see you work your magic. They will hire you to keep an audience engaged, and they need to see that you can hold an audience's attention.

This can be accomplished most effectively with your speaker demo video, also known as a *'sizzle reel.'*

Many times, the difference between a free speaker and a for fee speaker, is how good you are on this video. Many hosting organizations expect to *try* you before they *buy* you by watching your video for themselves, for the committee who makes the hiring decision, and even in front of a sampling of your potential audience.

Many hosting organizations believe that when it comes to your sizzle reel; *"What you see is what you get!"*

You may choose to take that one step further, by also listing some of the high-profile clients and companies you may have spoken for, and by including pictures or video clips of those events. Again, don't be afraid to drop name, places and events.

A strategically placed photo on your web site of an influential audience member giving you a standing ovation, has the effect of giving a prospective booker confidence in your skills.

Be sure to use keywords that relate to the types of speeches and audiences you reach and either highlights or a full speaker's kit related to the topics that you cover and specific speeches that you give.

<u>On Every Day and in Every Way, be About Marketing.</u>
Becoming an excellent speaker with a lot of experience doesn't happen overnight. You need to go out and do the work.

Reach back to organizations where you spoke for free previously to see if they have other events with budgets. Watch organizations that have meetings regularly and solicit them for future meetings.

You want to make your book(s) and your speaking your brand. And you want to make your brand known across social media.

<u>Start With a Small Fee</u>
As you transition from free to paid, be willing to take a modest fee.

Speakers speak.

Whatever stage you are at in your paid speaking career, set your fee so you can get hired at least two to three times a month. This profession takes a lot of practice in front of live audiences. There is no substitute for practice.

Where allowed, you should sell product in the back of the room. Always get permission from your host prior to setting up back of the room sales or sales of any kind.

Having a book to offer not only supplements your income, but it adds credibility to you as a speaker. In fact, the two activities, writing and speaking, serve to validate each other.

You can also ask for the organization to do an email blast for you as additional compensation.

<u>Negotiate Well.</u>
Getting paid your value as a speaker may be even more difficult than transitioning to becoming a paid speaker. This means that you need to know how to negotiate. You may often have to get creative, realizing that cash payment isn't the only type of compensation.

As a professional, you must be willing to deliver above and beyond what you are compensated for. That is the key to being invited back or getting recommended.

Be willing to be creative with your fee, especially as you're starting out. Finding out what else your clients have of value, or what else is in their budget, before turning down a no-fee gig is critically important.

If you need a sizzle reel, and your host is filming your presentation, a conference that is willing to give you the raw footage of you on their main stage may be well worth waiving your fee.

Sometimes a no-fee gig has money for training but not for speakers, or they can buy books for everyone in the audience or something else of value.

If there is money in their budget for training, consider participating in a breakout session, if they are offered, where you may conduct a workshop based on the subject matter of your book. Be sure to offer back of the room sales at the end of the break out session if so permitted.

Also, consider that they may be able to connect you with sponsors who may sponsor your talk by having you mention them in some way during your speech.

As you are starting out, you may need to help the event planner be creative in finding money.

As you progress in your experience, you will always need to negotiate. The first day of *'meeting planner school,'* future meeting planners are taught to ask for a discount. It's just part of the business.

Don't fall for the *"We're a non-profit"* line; it doesn't mean that they have no money or budget. Tell them that in that case you are aware that, as a non-profit, they must set a high standard for getting value in their expenditures and that you are quite prepared to insure that you will deliver that value.

GLOSSARY

A4 (paper size)
A4 measures 210 × **297 millimeters** or 8.27 × 11.69
inches. In PostScript, its dimensions are rounded off to 595
× 842 points. Folded twice, an A4 sheet fits in a C6 size
envelope (114 × 162 mm).

Author brand
A strong **author brand** is a credible signal of quality to
book buyers, which means more authority, more influence,
and even premium pricing. As you increase the perceived
value of your personal **brand**, your **brand** equity rises.
Successful **authors** shape and manage readers'
perceptions by controlling the message.

Branding
The marketing practice of creating a name, symbol or
design that identifies and differentiates a product, service,
individual or organization from other products, services,
individuals or organizations.

Brick and mortar
Brick and mortar (also bricks and mortar or B&M) refers to
a physical presence of an organization or business in a
building or other structure. The term brick-and-mortar
business is often used to refer to a company that possesses
or leases retail stores, factory production facilities, or
warehouses for its operations.

Coffee-table books
A coffee table book is an oversized, usually hard-covered
book whose purpose is for display on a table intended for
use in an area in which one entertains guests and from

which it can serve to inspire conversation. Subject matter is predominantly non-fiction and pictorial (a photo-book).

Collaborator
A person who collaborates with another such as someone who works with another person or group. on a task or project.

Conversion protocol
The rule and syntax that governs a conversion application. Similar to grammar.

Corkboard-and-index-cards
In the writing platform, Scrivener, cork board and index cards let you work on several levels at once, for example for story outlining or other complex documents where you need to stay on top of things.

Digital publication
Digital or electronic publishing includes the digital publication of e-books, digital magazines, and the development of digital libraries and catalogues.

Dropbox
Dropbox is a file hosting service operated by American company Dropbox, Inc., headquartered in San Francisco, California, that offers cloud storage, file synchronization, personal cloud, and client software.

Editing
Editing is when you make changes, especially to a written document, that improve the finished product. A good English teacher will tell you that editing is just as important as writing.

Fiction
A fiction is a deliberately fabricated account of something.

It can also be a literary work based on imagination rather than on fact, like a novel or short story.

Font
A font is the specific style of text that's printed on a page or displayed on a computer screen.

Freeware
Software that is provided without charge

Galley proof
In printing and publishing, galley proofs are the preliminary versions of publications meant for review by authors, editors, and proofreaders, often with extra-wide margins. Galley proofs may be uncut and unbound, or in some cases electronically transmitted.

HTML
Hypertext Markup Language is the standard markup language for creating web pages and web applications. With Cascading Style Sheets and JavaScript, it forms a triad of cornerstone technologies for the World Wide Web.

Intellectual property
Intellectual property is a category of property that includes intangible creations of the human intellect, and primarily encompasses copyrights, patents, and trademarks.

Literary agent query letter
A query letter is a one-page letter sent to literary agents in an effort to get them excited about your book. You have one page and 300 words (or less) to woo a literary agent into falling in love with your story and then requesting your manuscript. This letter is short, sweet, and definitely to the point.

Manga
Manga are comics created in Japan or by creators in the
Japanese language, conforming to a style developed in
Japan in the late 19th century. They have a long and
complex pre-history in earlier Japanese art.

Manuscript
A manuscript was, traditionally, any document written by
hand -- or, once practical typewriters became available,
typewritten -- as opposed to being mechanically printed or
reproduced in some indirect or automated way. The term
also applies to those documents created using a computer.

Media kit
A media kit is a package containing documents and other
promotional items about your business, product or event.
They are mainly used at events and for launches as a
package of information for journalists to help them write
their story.

Nonfiction
Non-fiction or nonfiction is content whose creator, in good
faith, assumes responsibility for the truth or accuracy of
the events, people, or information presented.

Novel
A novel is a relatively long work of narrative fiction,
normally in prose, which is typically published as a book.

One sheet
In the publishing and entertainment industries, a one-
sheet or one sheet is a single document that summarizes a
product for publicity and sales.

Open-source software
Open-source software is a type of computer software whose
source code is released under a license in which the

copyright holder grants users the rights to study, change, and distribute the software to anyone and for any purpose.

PDA
Personal digital assistant is a term for a small, mobile, handheld device that provides computing and information storage and retrieval capabilities for personal or business use, often for keeping schedules, calendars and address book information handy.

PDF
The Portable Document Format is a file format developed in the 1990s to present documents, including text formatting and images, in a manner independent of application software, hardware, and operating systems.

Pen name
An assumed name used by a writer instead of their real name. Mark Twain is the pen name of Samuel Langhorne Clemens.

Plagiarism
Plagiarism is the "wrongful appropriation" and "stealing and publication" of another author's "language, thoughts, ideas, or expressions" and the representation of them as one's own original work.

POD publishing
Print-on-demand is a printing technology and business process in which book copies are not printed until the company receives an order, allowing prints of singular or small quantities.

Proofreading
Proofreading means scrutinizing a written document in order to identify and rectify grammar, punctuation, spelling and vocabulary errors.

Sidebar
A narrow vertical area that is located alongside the main display area, typically containing related information or navigation options.

Sizzle reel
Sizzle reels (also commonly referred to as demo reels, promo videos, promotional videos, pitch reels, corporate communications video, media campaign video, montage videos, or media highlight reels) are 3-to-5 minute videos that combine visuals, audio, and messaging to create a fast.

Styles
A style is a collection of formatting instructions. You use styles to format the paragraphs in your document. So you would use the "Title" style for your title, "Body Text" style for body text, "Caption" style for the picture captions, and "Heading 1" for the major headings.

Subtitle
A subordinate title of a published work or article giving additional information about its content.

Trim size
The final size of a printed page after excess edges have been cut off is the trim size. Commercial printing companies often print several copies of one document on the same large sheet of paper. ... Then the company trims the large sheet down to the finished size of the printed piece—the trim size.

URL
A Uniform Resource Locator, colloquially termed a web address, is a reference to a web resource that specifies its location on a computer network and a mechanism for retrieving it.

WYSIWYG
WYSIWYG is an acronym for "what you see is what you
get". In computing, a WYSIWYG editor is a system in
which content can be edited in a form closely resembling
its appearance when printed or displayed.

Other Books by
Calvin G. Sims, Sr.

When The Student is Ready, the Teacher Will Appear

Intercellular Glutathione

Lawman: The Bass Reeves Story

Johnny Clem: 9 Year Old Hero of the Civil War

A Tale of Two Heroes: Mexico's Benito Juarez and America's Abraham Lincoln

Brother to Brother: Black Men Speak to Young Black Men (contributing author)

The Calvin Sims Story (Editor & Publisher)

Credit Repair, Yes YOU Can!

Turning TO Into FOR: Instead of asking God, "Why did you do this to me, as why did you do this for me?"

Relentless Winners: In Person and in Principle

What to Do and How to Do It: A Guide to Sustainable, Adult Independent Living in America (5 volumes)

- *Book 1*
- *Book 2*
- *Workbook 1*
- *Workbook 2*
- *Teacher's Guide*

The Overachiever's Handbook: Setting Your Own Expectations

For more information on Calvin G. Sims, Sr. please visit: http://www.calvinsims.com.

9 781717 884527